D1325796

ASCENDING LIABILITY

MERCER STUDIES IN LAW AND RELIGION 2

ASCENDING LIABILITY IN RELIGIOUS AND OTHER NONPROFIT ORGANIZATIONS

by

EDWARD MCGLYNN GAFFNEY, JR.
and
PHILIP C. SORENSEN

edited by

HOWARD R. GRIFFIN

CENTER FOR CONSTITUTIONAL STUDIES
AND
MERCER UNIVERSITY PRESS

ISBN 0-86554-153-1

ASCENDING LIABILITY IN RELIGIOUS
AND OTHER NONPROFIT ORGANIZATIONS
COPYRIGHT ©1984
MERCER UNIVERSITY PRESS, MACON GA 31207
ALL RIGHTS RESERVED
PRINTED IN THE UNITED STATES OF AMERICA

ALL BOOKS PUBLISHED BY MERCER UNIVERSITY PRESS
ARE PRODUCED ON ACID-FREE PAPER THAT EXCEEDS
THE MINIMUM STANDARDS SET BY THE
NATIONAL HISTORICAL PUBLICATIONS AND RECORDS COMMISSION.

LIBRARY OF CONGRESS CATALOGING IN PUBLICATION DATA
Gaffney, Edward McGlynn.
Ascending liability in religious
and other nonprofit organizations
(Mercer studies in law and religion)
Includes bibliographical references.
1. Corporations, Nonprofit—United States.
2. Corporations, Religious—Law and legislation—
United States.   3. Limited liability—United States.
4. Liability (Law)—United States.   I. Sorensen,
Philip C.   II. Griffin, Howard R., 1955-
III. Title.   IV. Series.
KF1388.G34   1984   346.73'064   84-22823
                       347.30664
ISBN 0-86554-153-1 (alk. paper)

CONTENTS

FOREWORD

When the out-of-court settlement of the *Barr* case ("Pacific Homes") was announced, there was a public outcry from certain ecclesiastical bodies. These were groups that had been disturbed by a growing number of theoretical legal questions and actual civil suits related to ascending liability principles. National and local religious groups and related nonprofit organizations suddenly felt threatened in a manner they had not previously experienced. Whether motivated by panic or resolve, many religious organizations hastily acted to prevent the many interpretations, implications, and applications stemming from the California case from violating their rights or infringing on their concerns. Hurriedly, agency executives consulted with their legal counselors, boards of trustees reexamined their constitutions and bylaws, and lawyers retained by denominational bodies pored over the rapidly emerging literature related to ascending liability cases.

Actually, until now, most law has been oriented to the for-profit rather than to the nonprofit sector of society. Understandably, courts have been unaware of the many subtle but substantive variations in ecclesiastical structures, typically regarding every religious group as either congregational or hierarchical.

Numerous religious bodies have recognized the dangers inherent in the influence of the *Barr* case. They have employed carefully researched secular interpretations of legal policy as well as historically affirmed internal convictions about ecclesiastical structure and polity to shape their actions accordingly.

In September 1981 the Executive Committee of the Southern Baptist Convention created and funded the Southern Baptist Convention Legal Affairs Committee. Its general assignment was to study ascending liability issues related to Southern Baptists. But it was also to explore the means by which it might cooperate with the Center for Constitutional Studies (then located at Notre Dame University) on an ecumenically oriented study project examining ascending liability. The materials found on the following pages represent the fruits of that research.

In a broad study of this nature, certain sectarian idiosyncrasies, structural subtleties, and nuances of denominational polity—easily discernible by persons involved in a particular faith but virtually unnoticeable to outsiders—could not be addressed in detail. Thus, individual religious organizations will do well to respond to this important overview with internal memoranda or white papers that address their own unique concerns. Three examples are offered from Methodist, Lutheran, and Baptist perspectives.

A certain amount of risk is involved in participating in a research project that evaluates—by referring to an emerging body of law and negligible precedence—denominational structures and programs of ministry based on theological convictions. Certainly, the church aspires to responsible citizenship in its involvement in social relationships and obedience to government policies. Yet, in good conscience, the church resists legal declarations that threaten to force a compromise of faith. Both church and society will suffer if the continuation of ministries prompted by compassion—ministries often involving risks—is stopped short by the nervous calculation of legal liabilities. The behavior of the church in society must be shaped by both its legal identity and its theological beliefs.

Many questions merit continued attention from a perspective appreciative of legal values and responsibilities and sensitive to the relationship between polity and doctrines, structures and ministries. Can government agencies regulate matters of church polity so as to alter the organizational pattern of entire denominations? How important is the issue of descending liability in present discussions about ascending liability? Generalizations and simplistic answers must be avoided in order that the diversity of our religious structures may be preserved. The traditional congregational, hierarchical, and presbyterial forms of denominational organization may no longer be adequate. Thus, stereotyped categorizations of religious groups must be avoided.

Studies such as this one and the dialogues provoked by it represent far more than an academic luxury of theoretical speculation. Already the practical stakes are high. The cases now before various courts are real. Radical results of actions now in process could include major denominational reorganizations with accompanying significant alterations in strategies and programs for missions.

Today it is no easier than it was in the first century to know how to render to Caesar what is Caesar's and to God what is God's. But, with the help of insights like those that follow, we must keep trying—for the good of society, for the benefit of persons in need, and for the glory of God.

C. Welton Gaddy, Chairman
Southern Baptist Convention
Legal Affairs Commitee

PREFACE

The law applicable to nonprofit organizations generally has been interpreted under the Model Nonprofit Corporation Act, which scarcely reaches the special area of law known as ascending liability. Professors Sorensen and Gaffney review the subject matter of ascending liability both generally, as the concept affects nonprofit corporations, and specifically, as this developing body of law concerns religiously affiliated institutions and agencies. Their work began in 1982 with primary emphasis on research methods designed to produce legal scholarship for publication in scholarly journals and periodicals of the legal profession. Further, their work was divided between research of nonprofit corporations generally, by Professor Sorensen, and religiously affiliated agencies, by Professor Gaffney. Professor Gaffney further approached the subject with emphasis on constitutional issues.

The editor, Howard Griffin, is responsible for integrating the authors' works and for adding in an appendix the denominational perspectives provided by Kent M. Weeks, Methodist; Philip E. Draheim, Lutheran; and James P. Guenther, Baptist.

The responsibility of nonprofit corporations for damages they may inflict upon others, and the problem, as posed by Professor Sorensen, is that the law provides greater relief for limiting liability to for-profit corporations and their wholly owned subsidiaries than to nonprofit corporations in business not to make money but to serve society. Sorensen observes that in certain circumstances a higher degree of liability attaches to nonprofit corporations. He subsequently presents his own solutions for desired changes in the law.

Professor Gaffney examines the subcomponent of nonprofit corporations that are religiously motivated or affiliated. He notes related problems that arose in the past and before the demise of charitable immunity. From that era he finds that individuals never thought to sue their own church and contrasts that position with the current trend of persons who sue the church for a variety of reasons, including abrogations of civil rights laws, torts, contracts, and the like. The body of case law examined in this portion suggests that although churches should not feel exempt from responsibility for damage they inflict upon others any more than should other large corporations, neither should the government, through the agency of the court, redefine the self-understanding of such religious bodies. Gaffney further points out that such problems become acute when a religious group's position is "congregational," and the courts attempt to shift such understandings to some connectional polity. For solving this problem the suggestion is made that courts become aware of the need for religious bodies to maintain their autonomy and integrity, free from intrusion by governmental and judicial bodies acting strictly to give relief to a plaintiff.

Ascending liability, as treated by both authors and as addressed in Dr. Gaddy's Foreword, is clearly an ecumenical problem experienced by all churches, other religious agencies, and nonprofit corporations of various forms and structures. A strong witness to such ecumenical and interreligious interests may be seen from the wide variety of groups supporting this project and representing various forms of denominational structure—congregational, presbyterial, and hierarchical.

The Center for Constitutional Studies is pleased to offer *Ascending Liability in Religious and Other Nonprofit Organizations* as the second publication in the series, Mercer Studies in Law and Religion. The authors, Professors Edward McGlynn Gaffney, Jr., and Phillip C. Sorensen, have contributed with this volume not only an important, seminal study but have added immeasurably to the growing body of law on this subject. Practitioners, administrators, jurists, scholars, churchmen, and laymen will benefit greatly from the publication of this work.

The editor, Howard R. Griffin, is directly responsible for the final manuscript and its organization. His efforts could not have contributed more to the excellence of the publication and the ease with which original and complex material was introduced.

Finally, there is no distinction without reader appreciation for the product. We at the Center for Constitutional Studies of Mercer University encourage your use and evaluation of this project.

W. Newton Moore, Esq.,
Executive Director, Center for Constitutional Studies
Chairman, John A. Sibley Institute for Public Affairs

ACKNOWLEDGMENTS

Mercer University and the Center for Constitutional Studies gratefully acknowledge the financial support of the following ecumenical bodies as well as other foundation and associational assistance: Christian College Coalition; Education Commission, Southern Baptist Convention; Executive Committee, Southern Baptist Convention; General Conference of Seventh-Day Adventists; Knights of Columbus; Mennonite Board of Missions; Patrick and Aimee Butler Family Foundation; Board of Higher Education and Ministry, United Methodist Church; General Council on Finance and Administration, United Methodist Church; Board of Global Ministries, United Methodist Church.

Further acknowledgment is made to the following individuals for special research applicable to the manuscript and for advice and guidance during the preparation of this project: Paul J. Bankes, attorney, Philadelphia, Pennsylvania; Wilfred R. Caron, general counsel, U.S. Catholic Conference; Philip E. Draheim, attorney, St. Louis, Missouri; Dr. Welton Gaddy, chairman, Southern Baptist Convention Legal Affairs Committee; Rabbi Michael Greenbaum, Jewish Theological Seminary of America; James P. Guenther, attorney, Nashville, Tennessee; J. Victor Hahn, Lutheran Council in the USA; Warren L. Johns, attorney, Washington, D.C.; W. Newton

Moore, director, Center for Constitutional Studies, Mercer University; Philip R. Moots, attorney, Columbus Ohio; J. Stuart Showalter, Catholic Health Association of the USA; Kent M. Weeks, attorney, Nashville, Tennessee.

Special credit and appreciation is extended to the authors and editor of the *Ascending Liability* manuscript: Edward McGlynn Gaffney, Jr., James P. Bradley Professor of Constitutional Law, Loyola Law School, Los Angeles, former director of the Center for Constitutional Studies (1981-1983); Howard R. Griffin, attorney, Civil Rights Division, United States Department of Justice, Washington, D.C., consultant and writer in education law, and former member of the research staff of the National Association of College and University Attorneys; Philip C. Sorensen, professor of law, Ohio State University, Columbus, Ohio.

I

AFFILIATIONAL ISSUES

Limiting exposure to liability is a major objective of entrepreneurs. The legal design of forms of association has been the product, in large part, of the tension between this goal and the competing goals of association creditors and claimants.[1] In general, profit-seeking entrepreneurs have been successful in limiting their liability through the use of forms of association that both separate and distance them from the enter-

---

[1]See Dodd, *The Evolution of Limited Liability in American Industry: Massachusetts*, 61 Harv. L. Rev. 1351 (1984); *see also* Gower, *Some Contrasts Between British and American Corporation Law*, 69 Harv. L. Rev. 1369 (1956); Note, *The Limited Partnership*, 45 Yale L.J. 895 (1936); Stevens, *Limited Liability in Business Trusts*, 7 Cornell L.Q. 116 (1922).

prise.[2] Entrepreneurs in the nonprofit sector, however, have not been as successful as their profit-making counterparts. Nonprofit associational forms that can provide the assurance of limited liability are neither numerous nor clear-cut. The problem is particularly acute among affiliated nonprofit organizations where one organization may be held responsible for the liabilities of another—a result referred to by many in the nonprofit sector as *ascending liability*, although the direction of extension may be other than up.[3]

The extension of liability from a nonprofit organization to an associated group cannot be fully addressed without considering the liability of a nonprofit organization for the acts of individuals. The ties to a nonprofit organization, as to a profit organization, are not altered by whether the related party is a person or another association. Thus the problem identified as ascending liability evinces the more general problem of the liability of nonprofit organizations for the acts of others. Relationships between two or more organizations, however, tend to be more complex and thereby more susceptible to misinter-

---

[2]"Limited liability" implies *some* exposure to liability, that exposure being the limited parties' investment in the separate identity carrying on the enterprise.

[3]For example, descending liability has occurred, as between related corporations, in workmen's compensation cases. *See, e.g., Boggs v. Blue Diamond Co.*, 590 F.2d 655 (6th Cir.), *cert. denied*, 444 U.S. 836 (1979). Lateral liability was sought in litigation culminating in the decision in *NAACP v. Claiborne Hardware Co.*, 458 U.S. 886 (1982). (Plaintiffs sought to freeze the bank accounts of all Mississippi chapters of the NAACP by naming 52 banks as "attachment defendants" even though only one chapter was claimed to be involved in the activities upon which liability was sought to be grounded.) *See* collateral proceedings in *Henry v. First National Bank of Clarksdale*, 50 F.R.D. 251 (N.D. Miss. 1970), *rev'd*, 444 F.2d 1300 (5th Cir. 1971), *cert. denied*, 405 U.S. 1019 (1972). Both descending and lateral liability may arise when related organizations are viewed as part of a larger and indivisible enterprise. *See* Berle, *The Theory of Enterprise Entity*, 47 Colum. L. Rev. 343 (1947).

pretation. Moreover, they cannot always be duplicated in the relationship between an individual and an organization.

The wholesale transfer of agency and liability principles from the profit to the nonprofit area without adequate consideration of differences in associational forms, motives, and relationships can result in unequal and unexpected outcomes.[4] Moreover, the flexibility of nonprofit groups to adapt to increased risk exposure by altering their relationships is not as great as for profit organizations. In many nonprofit organizations the need for, and nature of, the relationships of affiliates may be an inherent part of the enterprise (for example, a church denomination, the NCAA, the Farm Bureau, or the Democratic party). The structure and ties are ordinarily not determined by "bottom-line trade-offs." Although there is no evidence indicating an intention to treat nonprofit organizations differently, the state of current law renders them more vulnerable to ascending liability than similarly situated profit organizations.

The rules for determining the liability of a party for the unauthorized acts of another reflect an accommodation between the competing considerations of not "making one pay for another man's wrong"[5] and the justifications for doing so—risk spreading, a deep pocket, the prevention of harm, the concomitance of profit, and the responsibility for creation or

---

[4]The law for nonprofit organizations generally duplicates or parallels that of profit organizations. For example, the Model Nonprofit Corporation Act closely parallels, by intention, the Model Business Corporation Act. Indeed, the Nonprofit Corporation Act was prepared by the same committee (composed of business lawyers) that prepared the Business Corporation Act. *See* foreword to the 1952 edition of the Model Nonprofit Corporation Act, and preface to the 1953 revision of the Model Business Corporation Act. The parallels in organization structure and function, however, are more apparent than real.

[5]Holmes, *Agency*, 5 Harv. L. Rev. 1, 14 (1891).

control of forces leading to a cost. Liability may be either direct or vicarious.[6] The justifications for extending liability to the remote party fall into two broad, though not wholly separate, categories. The first and more traditional category extends liability by reason of causation[7] (that is, control or reliance) or by reason of the remote party's benefit from the actions of the actor. The second category justifies the extension of liability by reason of the remote party's ability to absorb the loss (that is, a deep pocket) or to better administer the risk (that is, avoid, prevent, shift, or distribute the loss).[8]

None of the latter justifications, however, standing alone, supports the extension of liability to a remote party. Indeed, while these grounds reinforce the traditional justifications and tend to push them toward their other limits, they have contributed little to the formulation of common-law, liability-extending rules and have provided little guidance in determining specific cases. The doctrine of enterprise liability,[9] for example, rather than being based on a notion of eco-

---

[6]Directly, a remote party may become liable, among other ways, by reason of a duty to supervise as a guarantor for the actions of another or through strict liability for a product or service to which the remote party contributed a part. Vicariously, the remote party may become liable through corporate veil piercing, through being part of an enterprise in which the participants are mutual agents for each other, as a principal in an agency relationship, or as a result of the application of those reliance doctrines of apparent authority, estoppel, or inherent agency.

[7]*See* Seavey, *Speculations as to "Respondeat Superior,"* Harvard Legal Essays, 433, 435-37 (1934), in which he states that vicarious liability is devoid of blameful conduct but not causation.

[8]*See* Douglas, *Vicarious Liability and Administration of Risk*, 38 Yale L. J. 584 (1929). For more contemporary analyses, *see, e.g.*, Kornhauser, *An Economic Analysis of the Choice Between Enterprise and Personal Liability for Accidents*, 70 Calif. L. Rev. 1345 (1982).

[9]Enterprise liability is the expression applied to the doctrines of *res-*

nomic efficiency, is grounded chiefly in the idea of responsibility arising from an enterprise's right to control and profit from its activities. Berle's theory of enterprise entity and enterprise-wide liability,[10] which disregards the artificial legal entities and looks at the actual "economic enterprise-fact," would otherwise, by now, have prevailed.

In contrast, the traditional justifications have established and shaped the various rules for extending liability. The common-law rules of agency, vicarious liability, limited liability, veil-piercing, and strict liability are, on the whole, refinements of those arguments. They cannot be said to disregard the economic arguments, but their design remains essentially moral.[11] That is to say, they do not impose liability upon a remote party absent a relationship containing elements of control and profit, or reliance upon representations of such a relationship.

1. OVERVIEW OF NONPROFIT ASCENDING LIABILITY CASE LAW

The basic legal principles for extending or limiting liability in and between profit organizations are reasonably well established, if not always well drawn or defined. Doctrines of

---

pondeat superior, product liability, joint venture, and strict liability, which hold an enterprise liable for the risks of its activities. *See, e.g.*, Steffin, *Enterprise Liability: Some Exploratory Comments*, 17 Hastings L.J. 165 (1965).

[10]Berle, *The Theory of Enterprise Entity*, 47 Colum. L. Rev. 343 (1947). Berle's theory has found some support, however, in regulatory situations. *See, e.g., NLRB v. Deena Artware, Inc.*, 361 U.S. 398 (1960); *United States v. J.B. Williams Co.*, 498 F.2d 414 (2d Cir. 1974). And for further support of the theory, *see* Landers, *A Unified Approach to Parent, Subsidiary, and Affiliate Questions in Bankruptcy*, 42 U. Chi. L. Rev. 589 (1975).

[11]The ties between the pragmatic and traditional arguments were never better demonstrated than in Douglas, *Vicarious Liability and Administration of Risk* (I & II), 38 Yale L.J. 584 (1929).

vicarious and limited liability, agency and partnership, control and authority, estoppel, and piercing the corporate veil have long been applied to, examined, and evaluated for profit organizations. Because of the more restricted activities of nonprofit organizations, a greater reluctance in the past to sue them, and the doctrine of charitable immunity, liability-extending rules have been less extensively applied or examined in the nonprofit context—especially as between related, nonprofit organizations. With the erosion of charitable immunity and many of the attitudes underlying that doctrine, however, courts increasingly have applied liability-extending doctrines to nonprofit organizations. The lawsuit that has brought the issue of ascending liability to the attention of nonprofit organizations, especially religious denominations, is *Barr v. United Methodist Church*,[12] also known as the "Pacific Homes" case.

The historic character of the *Barr* litigation was noted in the petition submitted to the United States Supreme Court for a writ of certiorari: "This is the first time in history that a major international religious denomination has been held to be suable as an 'unincorporated association.' "[13] Although the *Barr* case was eventually settled out of court, both the comprehensiveness and the novelty of the claims raised in the case make it appropriate to provide a detailed exploration of this important litigation.

Pacific Homes Corporation, a California nonprofit corporation, operated fourteen retirement homes. When the corporation filed for bankruptcy in 1978, Frank T. Barr and about 1,900 present and former residents of the homes brought a class-action suit against the corporation (hereafter

---

[12]*Barr v. United Methodist Church*, 90 Cal. App. 3d 259, 153 Cal. Rptr. 322 (1979), hereinafter cited as *Barr*.

[13]Petition for Cert. at 2, *Barr v. United Methodist Church*, No. 70-245 (1979).

Pacific Homes), the Pacific and Southwest Annual Conference of the United Methodist Church (PSWAC), the General Council on Finance and Administration of the United Methodist Church (GCFA), and the United Methodist Church (UMC).[14]

Pacific Homes had promised to provide lifetime care, including medical, nursing, and convalescent care, accommodations and, in most instances, food service in return for full prepayment or defined monthly payments for life by the residents. Since the retirement homes were unable to meet their obligations under the continuing-care agreements after Pacific Homes went bankrupt, the residents sought either equitable relief, fulfillment of the contract by resumption of services formerly provided, or a payment of damages in restitution.

The plaintiffs alleged that all the defendant organizations were financially responsible for the operation of Pacific Homes, and that the Pacific Homes Corporation was the agent and alter ego of each of the other defendants, and had acted with their permission, knowledge, and consent, and within the scope of their authority.

The United Methodist Church was joined as a party defendant on the theory that the denomination was an unincorporated association, capable of suing and being sued under the California Code of Civil Procedure.[15] Challenging the court's jurisdiction, the United Methodist Church moved to quash service on the ground that the United Methodist Church was not a legal entity. Rather, the denomination as-

---

[14]*Barr*, 90 Cal. App. 3d at 262-263, 153 Cal. Rptr. at 325. Added later to the party defendants were the General Board of Global Ministries, a New York nonprofit corporation, and the Division of Health and Welfare Ministries, an Illinois nonprofit corporation.

[15]Cal. Code of Civ. Proc. §388(a): Any partnership or other unincorporated association whether organized for profit or not, may sue and be sued in the name which it has assumed or by which it is known.

serted that it was merely a loose connectional system, the lack of unified structure or centralized administration being a reflection of the religious beliefs of Methodism. Therefore, the imposition of jural status, with the resulting treatment of the UMC as a unified or corporate structure amenable to suit, would be an unconstitutional violation of the due process, free exercise, and establishment of religion provisions of the United States and California Constitutions.

The trial court agreed and quashed service on the denomination. It held that the UMC is not an unincorporated association because it has a connectional structure maintained through periodic conferences. Referring to the article on Methodism in the *Encyclopedia Britannica*,[16] the court concluded that "'The United Methodist Church' is no more than a 'spiritual confederation' and is not a jural entity or unincorporated association subject to suit under [the] Code of Civil Procedure. . . ."[17] The trial court judge, Ross G. Sharp, wrote in his order:

> A contrary ruling would effectively destroy Methodism in this country, and would have a chilling effect on all churches and religious movements by inhibiting the free association of persons of similar religious beliefs. If all members of a particular faith were to be held personally liable for the transgressions of their fellow churchmen, church pews would soon be empty and the pulpits of America silent.[18]

---

[16]"A respected unbiased source, 'The Encyclopedia Britannica,' 1959 Ed., Vol. 15, p. 358, states: 'Methodism has continued for more than two centuries to proclaim a freedom of spirit as opposed to the bondage of an organization, and its appeal has been based on the reality of a personal experience of spiritual emancipation through faith in Christ." *Barr*, 90 Cal. App. 3d at 262, n.2, 153 Cal. Rptr. at 324-325, n.2.

[17]*Id.*

[18]*Id.*

The Fourth District Court of Appeal of California reversed this ruling of the trial court, finding that amenability
to suit would not have "any effect other than to oblige [the
UMC] to defend itself when sued upon civil obligations it is alleged to have incurred,"[19] and that its concern about the chilling effect on church membership should have been
considered by the religious body before it became involved in
commercial affairs. Looking to legal precedents rather than to
ecclesiastical expertise, the court of appeal found that the
UMC was an unincorporated association because it fit within
judicial definitions of such associations. According to the
court of appeal, the criteria for identifying an entity as an unincorporated association are "no more complicated than (1) a
group whose members share a common purpose, and (2) who
function under a common name under circumstances where
fairness requires the group be recognized as a legal entity."[20]
Since it is evident that the many subunits of the Methodist
denomination are connected by a common name and purpose, the sole issue remaining for the California court was
whether its understanding of fairness required the result it
reached. The court observed: "Fairness includes those situations where persons dealing with the association contend their
legal rights have been violated. Formalities of quasi-corporate
organization are not required."[21] Focusing on the organization of the denomination, the court found that the Methodist
polity was hierarchical rather than congregational because its
governing structure had clearly defined operating and con-
ceptual levels of responsibility. It examined the denominational subunits and found their functions and powers to

---

[19]*Id.* at 274, 153 Cal. Rptr. at 332.

[20]*Id.* at 266, 153 Cal. Rptr. at 328.

[21]*Id.* at 266-67, 153 Cal. Rptr. at 328 (citations omitted).

equate smoothly with legal corporate terms. For example, the *Book of Discipline of the United Methodist Church* described the Council of Bishops as "the *corporate* expression of episcopal leadership in the Church."[22]

When the court considered the position of the General Council on Finance and Administration in the hierarchical structure of the church, it even hinted at duplicity in the denomination's various characterizations of that body. On the one hand, the court referred to the description of the GCFA as a nondiscretionary conduit rendering nondiscretionary auditing and financial service to some of the general level agencies. On the other hand, the court noted that in applying for a group tax exemption, the GCFA was described to the IRS as the "central treasury and fiscal agent of the UMC," authorized by the *Book of Discipline* " 'to take all necessary legal steps to safeguard and protect the interests and rights of the United Methodist Church.' A reasonable legal inference which can be drawn from this grant and description of authority to an agent is the existence of UMC as principal."[23]

In concluding that the denomination is a unified entity, the court described UMC as a highly organized religious body working through specific agencies to accomplish laudable goals. After reviewing the relationship between Pacific Homes and UMC, the court stated that the reason why the entire church should be regarded as a jural entity capable of being

---

[22]The *Book of Discipline*, para. 525 (1976), *quoted in Barr*, 90 Cal. App. 3d. at 268, 154 Cal. Rptr. at 329 (emphasis supplied). The court was apparently unaware of the biblical understanding of the central New Testament image of the Church as the body of Christ, for it used this provision of the *Book of Discipline* as evidence that the Council of Bishops is the functional equivalent of a corporate board of directors, in a formal legal sense, for the entire denomination.

[23]*Id.* at 269, 153 Cal. Rptr. at 329, *quoting Book of Discipline*, para. 843.3 (1976).

sued was that the church had chosen to undertake a social mission in the world:

> UMC, in fulfilling its commitment to society, has elected to involve itself in worldly activities by participating in many socially valuable projects. It has enjoyed the benefits, both economic and spiritual, of those projects. It has even on occasion filed suit for the protection of its interests. It must now, as part of its involvement in society, be amenable to suit.[24]

The church argued that the religion clauses of the First Amendment barred the court from examining denominational polity to determine whether the religious body was amenable to suit. Although acknowledging that disputes concerning ecclesiastical government should be resolved by religious tribunals, and that such decisions are normally binding on the civil courts, the court suggested that it was not bound by the finding of a religious body when a secular court is called upon to resolve a secular dispute. Such judicial deference in nonreligious disputes "would . . . grant immunity to religious organizations in cases which might arise far afield from religious activities."[25] Indeed, the *Barr* court suggested that in determining the jural status of an organization, to treat religious bodies by a different standard from one used for nonreligious organizations "in purely secular suits might very well constitute a preference for religion in violation of the establishment clause."[26]

The trial court had expressly ruled that the UMC could not be regarded as a jural entity amenable to suit on the ground that doing so would have a chilling affect not only on

---

[24]*Id.* at 272, 153 Cal. Rptr. at 331.

[25]*Id.* at 274, 153 Cal. Rptr. at 332.

[26]*Id.* at 275, 153 Cal. Rptr. at 333, *citing Abington School District v. Schempp*, 374 U.S. 208 (1963).

the UMC, but on all churches and religious movements. In overruling the trial court on this matter, the appellate court wrote that the UMC had offered no evidence to show that rendering UMC amenable to suit would affect the distribution of power or property within the denomination and suggested that the only effect of regarding the UMC as a jural entity would be to oblige UMC to defend itself when sued upon civil obligations it is alleged to have incurred. In short, the appellate court rejected the contention of the defendants that serious constitutional issues were presented in the *Barr* litigation:

> The statutory enactments involved in this action are for the purpose of providing substantive rights to citizens and to assure access to the courts, including the right to sue organizations functioning as unincorporated associations. The internal ecclesiastical judicial system of UMC does not provide any method of redress for plaintiffs. The use of the courts as a method of dispute resolution cannot be foreclosed to this class of plaintiffs who have alleged fraud, breach of contract and statutory violations because one of the named defendants is a religious body. Neither the State nor the Federal Constitution may be interpreted in a manner which would deny plaintiffs the right to sue UMC.[27]

The United States Supreme Court declined to review the *Barr* case,[28] and the case was eventually settled out of court. The precedent created by the appellate decision in this case could have important ramifications for all religious bodies, for it holds broadly that an entire denomination is a legal entity amenable to suit for the activities of affiliate organizations with which virtually any form of agency, sponsorship, or control can be found.

---

[27]*Id*. at 275-276, 153 Cal. Rptr. at 333.

[28]*UMC v. Barr*, No. 79-249, *cert. denied*, 444 U.S. 973 (1979).

The real significance of *Barr* is that the relationship between the United Methodist Church and Pacific Homes was not especially unusual. If the United Methodist Church and its denominational agencies could be liable for the contracts of Pacific Homes, then they and other denominations could be liable for the contracts and torts of thousands of schools, hospitals, homes, colleges, and agencies where the relationship is akin to that of Pacific Homes. The Pacific Homes case, then, has raised several open-ended questions concerning the legal responsibility of religious bodies for the actions taken by their agencies and affiliates, as well as the legal responsibility of these agencies and affiliates for each other.

The amount of the out-of-court settlement in *Barr* was twenty-one million dollars, and the legal fees incurred by the church and various boards or agencies involved in the suit were reported to have approximated four million dollars. Although the financial consequences of the ascending liability issue can be substantial, or even catastrophic in some instances, ascending liability is much more than a money issue to religious and other nonprofit organizations. The social impact of the *Barr* case will far exceed the cash settlement if these kinds of organizations choose, by reason of their new awareness of the extent of their risk exposure, to forgo sponsorship of socially beneficial programs or to restrict the activities of their agencies. Moreover, the structures and procedures of governance of nonprofit organizations might require profound alterations in order to protect against legal doctrines that permit unlimited ascending liability. A nonprofit group might have to choose between unlimited exposure to risk or a form of organization and governance incompatible with its tenets. Such a dilemma would be especially unpalatable to a religious body if the only form of organization and governance available to it to limit its liability were unacceptable as a matter of religious conviction.

A textbook example of nonprofit ascending liability is *NAACP v. Overstreet*.[29] In this suit by a merchant for damages arising out of a boycott led by the Savannah chapter of the NAACP, the jury found that the local branch acted as an agent for the Georgia State Conference of Branches and for the national NAACP, a New York corporation, and that the state and national organizations were thereby liable. On appeal, the Georgia Supreme Court said that the issue was not whether the president of the local was an agent for the state or national organizations, but whether the president of the local was the agent for either organization. According to the court, the record showed that the president was an agent for the national but not an agent for the state organization (although he was also president of the state organization). Later still, four Justices of the United State Supreme Court, in dissenting from a dismissal of an earlier grant of certiorari, could discover no evidence of agency among any of the parties.[30]

Overstreet raises a particularly perplexing issue relevant to many nonprofit organizations. Who is the principal and who the agent if the existence of agency is to be based on organizational relationships? The Georgia Supreme Court apparently perceived the NAACP locals and their members as nonautonomous agents of the national organization: "[T]he NAACP Corporation of New York acts and operates in Georgia through the Savannah Chapter and other chapters,"[31] and, "the locals are within the framework of the national organization and are used in furtherance of the latter's business and interest."[32] Actually, authority in the NAACP runs in both di-

---

[29]221 Ga. 16, 142 S.E.2d 816, *cert. granted*, 382 U.S. 937, *cert. dismissed*, 384 U.S. 118 (1965).

[30]384 U.S. at 125-26.

[31]221 Ga. at 26, 142 S.E.2d at 826.

[32]*Id.* at 27, 142 S.E.2d at 826.

rections—from the local to the national and vice versa[33]—and it is not implausible to view the national NAACP as an agent of the members. The Georgia Supreme Court is not alone, however, in equating authority with scope.[34] It is easy to assume and perceive a nonprofit, national organization to be the counterpart of the large, multinational business corporation with authority proceeding down from the top.

Overstreet also highlights the difficulty in the nonprofit context when dealing with the agency requirement that one party be acting "on behalf of" and "for the benefit of" another. The Georgia Supreme Court, in finding agency, spoke of the locals as acting in furtherance of the national's business and interest, which it earlier described as "giving aid and assistance to Negroes." The court in *Barr* perceived UMC as enjoying the benefits of projects such as retirement homes (and presumably orphanages, colleges, and hospitals). The United States Supreme Court saw the nonprofit American Society of Mechanical Engineers as benefiting from the work of its members in promulgating engineering and industrial advisory codes and standards.[35] And the California Supreme Court saw the conduct of a Bible school by a local Presbyterian church as

---

[33]The author was informed by the Midwest regional director of the NAACP that members of local NAACP chapters are automatically members of the national organization and send delegates to a national convention. These delegates elect some directors of the national NAACP and adopt national policy.

[34]*See, e.g., Barr*, 90 Cal. App. 3d 259, 153 Cal. Rptr. 322 (1979); the trial court result in *Pentecostal Holiness Church, Inc. v. Mauney*, 270 So. 2d 762 (Fla. Dist. Ct. App. 1972); the claims for plaintiffs in *Kersh v. General Council of the Assemblies of God*, 535 F.Supp. 494 (N.D. Cal. 1982); and *generally Crawley v. American Soc'y of Equity of North America*, 153 Wis. 13, 139 N.W. 734 (1913).

[35]*American Soc'y of Mech. Eng'rs v. Hydrolevel Corp.*, 456 U.S. 556, 576 (1982).

in "the interest of the . . . Presbytery."[36] These examples pose little problem if the actors are agents acting at the direction of the principal/organization, or if the task is one exclusively in furtherance of the objects of the principal/organization. But all works by affiliated parties that carry forward the ideals of the affiliated organizations do not necessarily serve to benefit, in an agency sense, those organizations. A member or affiliated organization of the national NAACP may not be acting to benefit the national organization when that member or affiliate acts, on its own initiative, to further the cause of blacks. A church member or church affiliate may not be acting to benefit the church or denomination by engaging in good works.

A further problem with agency concepts operating in the nonprofit context is portrayed by two recent lawsuits seeking to recover from Roman Catholic dioceses for the torts of parish priests.[37] Witnesses for the parties, experts in canon law, disputed the extent of the right of the bishop to exercise control over the priest. Plaintiffs' expert witness, a University of California law professor, took the position that a priest is at all times acting for the Church, a position that appears not to distinguish between the doctrinal control reposed in the bishop and the control generally required for a master-servant relationship.[38] The court in *Barr*, in suggesting a hierarchical Methodist church, did not distinguish between secular and spiritual authority in citing the *Book of Discipline*.[39]

---

[36]*Malloy v. Fong*, 37 Cal. 2d 356, 377, 232 P.2d 241, 253 (1951).

[37]*Stevens v. Roman Catholic Bishop*, 49 Cal. App. 3d 877, 123 Cal. Rptr. 171 (1975); *Ambrosio v. Price*, 495 F.Supp. 381 (D. Neb. 1979). *See also* Hotz, *Diocesan Liability for Negligence of a Priest*, 26 Cath. Law. 228 (1981).

[38]*See generally* Restatement (Second) of Agency § 220 (1957).

[39]*Barr*, 90 Cal. App. 3d at 267-70, 153 Cal. Rptr. at 328-30.

2. ORIGIN AND TYPES
OF DENOMINATIONAL POLITY

Doctrinal or ideological ties or commitments can, however, exist independently of the power to control conduct. Relationships based upon such ties or commitments, either wholly or in part, are common in the nonprofit sector. The structure by which a religious association implements religious doctrine is called its polity, or organizational pattern of governance. Polity establishes the relationships among the units and subunits in the denomination, and between the denomination itself and those units. The amount of responsibility or control that any element within the denomination may have for the acts of another element depends upon that polity.

Although there is great variety to be found in the patterns used to structure religious associations, three general categories of polity are usually offered. The first two, congregational and hierarchical, were described in *Watson v. Jones*[40] (described fully in chapter 2, subsection 1). The important characteristics of congregational polity are self-governance and equality. The local churches are autonomous, and church members have equal power in the determination of decisions of their congregation. Although local churches may interact with one another, each congregation "is strictly independent of other ecclesiastical associations, and so far as church government is concerned, owes no fealty or obligation to any higher authority."[41] Denominational bodies therefore may only advise congregations. Examples of major Christian denominations with this type of polity are Congregational, Uni-

---

[40]80 U.S. (13 Wall.) 679, 722-23 (1872).

[41]*Id.*, at 722.

tarian, Disciples of Christ, Baptist, Quaker, Churches of Christ, and some Adventist and Lutheran churches; Jewish congregations are also structured on this model of governance.[42]

The second category, hierarchical or episcopal, places power in clerical superiors. The local congregation is subordinate to higher church units and to an ecclesiastical tribunal with ultimate control. Examples of this type are Roman Catholic, Orthodox, Episcopal, and some Lutheran and Brethren churches.[43]

The third type, presbyterial, also called "synodal" or "connectional," blends characteristics of the other two kinds of polity. The local congregations are autonomous in directing their own activities. Each church, however, elects representatives who attend governing bodies of the denomination. The authority of the general church, therefore, is exercised by both lay representatives and ministers acting in an ascending succession of decision-making bodies, from local church to presbytery to synod to general assembly. Denominations with this type of structure include Presbyterian, Reformed Church in America, Evangelical and Reformed Church, Christian Reformed Church, and other Calvinist and some Lutheran churches.[44]

Because of the frequent reliance by courts on the *Watson* decision, both episcopal and presbyterial polities are usually combined into one category, hierarchical. However, even the division into three classes is an imprecise treatment. Another

---

[42]*See, e.g.*, Note, *Imposing Corporate Forms on Unincorporated Denominations: Balancing Secular Accountability With Religious Free Exercise*, 55 S. Cal. L. Rev. 155, 167 (1981) and Note, *Judicial Intervention in Disputes Over the Use of Church Property*, 75 Harv. L. Rev. 1142, 1143 (1962).

[43]Note, *Imposing Corporate Forms, supra* n.42, at 167.

[44]*Id.*

hybrid polity, containing "an eclectic form of organization with both presbyterial and episcopal characteristics,"[45] is seen in the Methodist denomination and in the Church of the United Brethren in Christ. But because ultimate authority is placed in superior units, they usually are considered hierarchical.

A denomination's polity usually is based upon its religious beliefs and is derived from historical or scriptural sources. The biblical references for a hierarchical structure are found in the roles assigned in the New Testament to various church officers, including elders (presbyters), overseers (episcopal leaders), the Twelve, the Apostles, and the Petrine office of nurturing and caring for the Christian community in some unique way.

Congregational polity emphasizes the independence of each church. The congregation rules itself as a voluntary association that owes an allegiance only to Christ. It is believed that the spirit of Jesus manifests itself in the conviction of each individual believer, and that his influence is felt through the church members. Thus, Christ's authority guides the local churches through individuals in the congregation. This type of arrangement follows closely the structure of some of the earliest Christian communities in the Hellenistic world of the first century. Paul's letter to the Corinthians, for example, appears to be addressed to a small, self-governed group limited in membership to those who were close enough to the meeting place, and led by ministers and deacons chosen among themselves; on the other hand, it is clear even in these very early writings that Paul maintained apostolic authority over the communities that he founded.

The same scriptural and historical references are generally recognized by denominations with presbyterial polity, which blend characteristics found in the hierarchical and con-

---

[45]Note, *Judicial Intervention, supra* n.42, 75 Harv. L. Rev. at 1144, n.14.

gregational structures. Local churches keep their independent and autonomous responsibilities. However, the belief in
the whole church of Christ creates a spiritual unification
which has led to the affiliation of geographically related
churches for fellowship and some administrative purposes.
Their democratic methods of association have also grown
from the New Testament church structures, which in turn followed somewhat the governance of the Jewish synagogues in
the Hellenistic world.

Thus, the polities of all three denominational categories
have biblical roots in the history of the early church. Although
from the earliest period of Christianity secular influences also
affected the structural development of a given community, the
choice of polity grew largely from a desire that the denomination be able to fulfill its scripturally mandated obligations
and religious tenets. These organizational patterns may or
may not fit comfortably into a secular structural form like the
modern corporation. Nevertheless, governmental structure
has been imposed on religious bodies throughout America's
history.

3. THE NONPROFIT DISTINCTION

Is there reason to consider nonprofit groups separately?
Is "nonprofit" a useful classification of organizations? The
term itself is not descriptive; it connotes what the organizations are not, and denotes all organizations other than profit
ones. Legally the term conveys only the information that organizational profits may not be distributed on a current basis
to controlling persons.[46] Does this incapacity constitute or cre-

---

[46]Hansmann defines a nonprofit organization as one "barred from
distributing its net earnings, if any, to individuals who exercise control over
it, such as members, officers, directors, or trustees." This prohibition he
terms the "nondistribution constraint." Hansmann, *The Role of Nonprofit
Enterprise*, 89 Yale L.J. 835, 838 (1980). *But see infra* n.47, for an exception
to this constraint.

ate any unifying theme? Are there other traits common to nonprofit organizations?

If there is a nonprofit organizational consanguinity, none has been shown. The vast diversity of nonprofit organizations pursuing both public and private interests evidences no common denominator. The limitation on profit distribution apparently limits little else, including profit making.[47] Professor Hansmann has contended that the incapacity to distribute profits makes nonprofit organizations relatively more trustworthy and thereby responsive to a particular marketplace.[48] Currently, however, there is little more to support his thesis than "casual empiricism"—an academic form of judicial notice—and Hansmann himself notes nonprofit social clubs as an exception.[49]

The absence of uniform characteristics among nonprofit organizations does not, however, invalidate the profit/nonprofit distinction. While it is inappropriate to formulate rules for nonprofit organizations as a class if they have nothing in common, it is injudicious to assume that rules made for profit organizations are equally suitable to nonprofit groups. The incapacity of nonprofit organizations—which would be better labeled as all organizations other than profit ones—to distribute profits is not their only distinctive trait. Other structural and functional differences, although not invariably present, do exist that make the usual underlying premises of liability-extending rules inapposite. Four immediate associational differences should be noted.

---

[47]A nonprofit organization may earn a profit and in some jurisdictions pass on those profits to members through the distribution of assets on dissolution. *See* Hansmann, *Reforming Nonprofit Corporation Law*, 129 U. Pa. L. Rev. 497, 574-80 (1981). Thus, the term *nonprofit* is doubly misleading.

[48]Hansmann, *The Role of Nonprofit Enterprise*, 89 Yale L.J. 835 (1980).

[49]*Id*. at 892.

A. *Forms of Association*

While there are four basic forms of profit association—the corporation, the general partnership, the limited partnership, and the business trust—there are essentially only two forms of nonprofit association, the nonprofit corporation and the unincorporated association.[50] The smaller number of nonprofit forms is more than a curiosity, for it has bearing on the significance to be assigned to the choice of form by a nonprofit group, in the flexibility of nonprofit groups when dealing with shortcomings of particular associational forms, and in the aptness of organizational analogies between profit and nonprofit groups. There should perhaps be additional forms of nonprofit organization, but borrowed principles and policies may not always fit the limited number of nonprofit forms.

B. *Members, Shareholders, and Partners*

Members of nonprofit corporations are often viewed or treated as the equivalent of shareholders in profit organizations.[51] It is true that the rights and duties of members may parallel those of shareholders; for example, members may

---

[50]The cooperative is omitted because, in a qualified way, it is a profit organization. To the extent that it can be said to be a nonprofit enterprise, the cooperative presents no distinctive traits pertinent to this discussion. Nonprofit or charitable trusts are omitted because, when unincorporated, they function, unlike the business trust, as passive instruments rather than as operating associations.

[51]Internal Revenue Code § 501(c)(3)(1954), for example, uses the term *shareholder* as if synonymous with *member* when providing an exemption for charitable and other organizations so long as no net earnings inure "to the benefit of any private shareholder or individual." Requests by members for inspection of nonprofit corporation records or member lists have, on occasion, been treated as raising no different issues than a shareholder's request to inspect a profit corporation's records. For a discussion of the distinctive issues, however, *see* Nida, *Membership Lists; Balancing the Interests Between Use and Abuse*, 13 U.S.F. L. Rev. 797 (1979).

have the power to elect the board of directors, amend the charter, share in the benefits of the organization, and yet be screened from involvement in the day-to-day management of the association. This possibility for equivalent rights and duties, however, should not be extended into a full-blown analogy.

Members can possess interests and rights greater or lesser than shareholders. The Model Nonprofit Corporation Act[52] defines members simply as those "having membership rights"[53] with membership rights consisting of those "set forth in the articles of incorporation or the by-laws."[54] Membership can arise from serving on the board of directors[55] or from no more than being a customer or contributor.[56] Members may,

---

[52]Model Nonprofit Corp. Act (1964).

[53]*Id.* at § 2(f).

[54]*Id.* at § 11.

[55]"Where neither the articles nor the regulations provide for members . . . the trustees shall, for the purposes of any statute or rule of law relating to corporations, be taken to be the members of such corporation." Ohio Rev. Code Ann. § 1702.14 (Baldwin 1979). Many states have similar provisions.

[56]Ellman has pointed out that the term *member* is used sometimes in the corporate-law sense and sometimes to signify entitlements or recognition unrelated to governance or control of the organization. Ellman, *Another Theory of Nonprofit Corporations*, 80 Mich. L. Rev. 999, 1011 n.34 (1982). For an example of the latter use of the term *member, see Federal Election Comm'n v. National Right to Work Committee*, 458 U.S. 1130 (1982), where the issue was what constituted membership within the meaning of The Federal Election Campaign Act of 1971, 2 U.S.C. § 441b(b)(4)(c). Although the National Right to Work Committee stated in its charter that it would have no members, it would send membership cards and newsletters to those who contributed or otherwise favorably responded to their mass-mail solicitations. The "members" played no part in the governance of the organization. The Court held them not to be members within the meaning of

by reason of their membership, exercise a management-like control over the organization, or may lack a participation in both the control and the benefits of the organization. Indeed, there may be neither members nor others holding a distinct, proprietary-like interest in a nonprofit organization, or the party holding that interest may be a nonmember.[57]

Procedures for becoming a member are often left unclear, as are procedures for terminating that status. Many persons may become unwitting members of a nonprofit organization, under that organization's bylaws, by subscribing to a magazine or making a donation.[58]

Members of nonprofit, unincorporated associations are sometimes compared to partners, but the analogy fails for reasons similar to those indicated above. Unlike partners, members of unincorporated associations may have no proprietary stake in the organization.[59] Moreover, members may join or re-

---

the Act. However, entitlements, such as magazine subscription, or recognition, such as for a donation, may be, under the Model Nonprofit Corporation Act, as much "membership rights" as the right to elect directors. California has addressed this dilemma by defining a member as any person who "has the right to vote for the election of a director. . . ." Cal. Corp. Code § 5056(a) (West Supp. 1980).

[57]A nonprofit organization need not be "owned." Indeed, the point is often made that charitable organizations have no owners except possibly the public. Nevertheless, nonprofit organizations, whether charitable or not, may have members who exercise control equivalent to that of owners.

[58]Members under the Model Nonprofit Corporation Act, *supra* n.52, are defined by the organization's intentions (as set forth in its governing instruments) rather than by the consent or intention of the putative member.

[59]A partnership is an association organized for profit (Uniform Partnership Act § 6) and partners are co-owners of, *inter alia*, profits, the right to participate in the management, and specific partnership property (Uniform Partnership Act §§ 24-26). Members of nonprofit, unincorporated associations may have no property interests or management rights if the articles of association or bylaws so provide.

sign most nonprofit organizations, whether incorporated or not, without affecting the continuity of the association and without the consent of the other members.[60]

C. Basis for Affiliation

Social, political, philanthropic, aspirational, or ideological reasons may form the basis for affiliation with a nonprofit association or participation in it. In profit organizations, the basis for affiliation will be, with few exceptions, pecuniary. A nonprofit organization may be as acquisitive as its profit counterpart, yet—and this is the point—it often is not. A nonprofit association may promote common interests, and while for some organizations those interests may be beneficial to the membership, for others they may be limited to selfless aspirations. Affiliation may involve a commitment of time and money or merely a signification of support for certain ideas or ideals without further obligation.

This absence of a pecuniary basis for affiliation is reflected in numerous court decisions choosing not to intervene in the internal affairs of nonprofit associations when no property interests are at stake.[61] Thus, relationships within all profit organizations, because of their pecuniary basis, will be legally fixed and judicially refereed while those relationships in nonprofit organizations founded upon nonpecuniary bases remain largely beyond judicial reach.

Moreover, relationships within and between nonprofit associations may be a matter of essence. A democratic form in a civil rights organization, a presbytery structure in a religious organization, a collegial structure in a university—these are

---

[60]To be a partner requires the consent of all other members. Uniform Partnership Act § 18(g). Membership does not require such consents unless the association's governing instruments require otherwise.

[61]*See* Chafee, *The Internal Affairs of Associations Not for Profit*, 43 Harv. L. Rev. 993 (1930); *Developments in the Law—Judicial Control of Actions or Private Associations*, 76 Harv. L. Rev. 983 (1963).

structures of affiliation that are not simply a part of an economic calculus, nor readily alterable for bottom-line considerations.[62]

D. Formality of Affiliation

Taxes, regulations, risk exposure, profit-distribution, and questions of control require a high degree of explicitness in profit-making relationships. Nonprofit organizations, being considerably less concerned with regulations and taxes, and not at all concerned with profit distribution, and being tied together through beliefs and social objectives, are likely to create informal, indistinct, and uncertain forms and systems of organization. Since many affiliations are neither fixed nor enforceable at law, the definition and documentation of those affiliations are likely to receive scant attention.

Moreover, the question of when concerted, noncommercial activity coheres into an association has, unlike concerted, commercial activity, received slight analysis. Two tests have been employed; one of *form* (that is, are there officers, a constitution, bylaws, and does it operate like an association?),[63]

---

[62]The structures of many religious organizations are directly tied to their religious beliefs. For the distinctive legal problems raised thereby *see* Morgan, *The Significance of Church Organizational Structure in Litigation and Government Action*, 16 Val. U.L. Rev. 145 (1981); Note, *Imposing Corporate Forms on Unincorporated Denominations: Balancing Secular Accountability with Religious Free Exercise*, 55 S. Cal. L. Rev. 155 (1981).

[63]*Hecht v. Malley*, 265 U.S. 144 (1924); *Georgia v. National Democratic Party*, 447 F.2d 1271 (D.C. Cir.), *cert. denied*, 404 U.S. 858 (1971); *Ripon Soc'y v. National Republican Party*, 525 F.2d 567 (D.C. Cir. 1975), *cert. denied*, 424 U.S. 933 (1976); *Hidden Lake Development Co. v. District Court*, 183 Colo. 168, 515 P.2d 632 (1973). In *Hecht*, the Court offers a number of definitions of associations, all of which require, *inter alia*, a form and procedure resembling a corporation. In *Hidden Lake Development Co.*, a loosely formed association of neighboring landowners was not permitted to sue as an unincorporated association solely on the assertion that it was one. An asso-

and the other of *common purpose* and fairness ("a group whose members share a common purpose . . . . where fairness requires the group to be recognized as a legal entity").[64] This latter test, applied in *Barr*,[65] creates unincorporated associations without, apparently, the consent or intention of those who would be held to be their members. While a partnership may be created by implication[66] from the conduct of the parties evidencing an intent to create a partnership, not even this prerequisite appears necessary for the creation of an unincorporated association under the common purpose/fairness test. Neither an agreement, nor an intention to form an association, nor an assertion that one exists, need be present.[67] The

---

ciation, the court said, is "usually characterized by having by-laws . . . , a stated purpose for its existence, and providing for its continuity though its membership may change. There should also be responsible officers elected according to the by-laws. . ." 515 P.2d at 635.

[64]"A group of persons acting together for a common purpose" appears to be the typical definition of an association in the common law and statutes, sometimes with the added requirement of a common name. Since this definition can potentially create an association out of a infinite number of coordinated or uncoordinated group actions that have been labeled by the participants or the public (*e.g.*, feminists, conservatives), more is needed for an association to be legally cognizable. Perhaps that "more" is grounded on ideas of fairness—even when it consists only of a requirement that the group, in form, resemble a corporate association. However, factors other than form have sufficed (*see, e.g., United Mine Workers of America v. Coronado Coal Co.*, 259 U.S. 344 (1922); *Teubert v. Wisconsin Interscholastic Athletic Ass'n*, 8 Wis. 2d 373, 99 N.W.2d 100 (1959). To date, these factors have received no characterization except fairness.

[65] Cal. App. 3d at 266, 153 Cal. Rptr. at 327.

[66]*See* H. Reuschlein & W. Gregory, *Handbook on the Law of Agency and Partnership* § 262 (1979).

[67]The formation of a partnership requires the presence of an express agreement, an agreement implied from conduct, or estoppel. *See* Uniform Partnership Act § 16.

common purpose/fairness test simply means that any concerted activity, so long as it is nonprofit, is susceptible to giving
birth to an association—and to the mutual agency implications thereof.[68] Moreover, since ties of affiliation are often informal and indistinct, the boundaries of an unincorporated
association can be extended judicially to encompass those with
the most tenuous of connections.

4. AFFILIATIONS
OF RELIGIOUS BODIES

State statutes gradually developed four means of incorporation for religious bodies.[69] Some states simply restruc-
tured the old British concept of special charter and granted a
charter to a religious corporation after procedural filings were
made. There were even special laws in some states for the incorporation of particular denominations.[70] Today the implication that a state might be bestowing a privilege on a
denomination has been removed; instead, the state accepts
properly filed articles of incorporation from any organization
wishing to be incorporated.

A method of incorporation adopted from the common
law by the early states (and still in use today) is the trustee cor-

---

[68]For the liability of members of an unincorporated association, *see* H.
Ford, *Unincorporated Non-profit Associations*, 51-69 (1959); Comment, *Liability of Members and Officers of Nonprofit Unincorporated Associations for Contracts and Torts*, 42 Calif. L. Rev. 812 (1954); Note, *Developments in the Law-
Judicial Control of Actions of Private Associations*, 76 Har. L. Rev. 983, 1008
(1963).

[69]Morgan, *The Significance of Church Organizational Structure in Litigation and Government Action*, 16 Val. U.L. Rev. 145, 145-153 (1981).

[70]New Jersey, for example, has both a general statute for incorporation
of religious societies and a specific one for incorporation of the Protestant
Episcopal church. N.J. Stat. Ann. § 16:12-4 (West 1976). *See* Morgan *supra*
n.69, 16 Val. U.L. Rev. at 149, n.25.

poration. The church trustees themselves were incorporated and held the property of the unincorporated church. Those assets were then perpetually held by successive trustees, rather than by the religious body, in trust either for particular beneficiaries or for a particular use or purpose. This theory of implied trust, known as Lord Eldon's Rule, was followed by some American courts. In a dispute over church property, the assets were awarded to the group that had not departed from the fundamental doctrines of the church. In making that determination, however, courts examined and passed judgment on basic church beliefs, in violation of the mandated separation between church and state.

In 1872 the Supreme Court abolished the rule for federal courts, rejecting both the implied trust and departure-from-doctrine concepts in the *Watson* case. As Justice Miller wrote in *Watson*, the ecclesiastical tribunal or internal governing body of the denomination must resolve internal church dispute, and their decisions are final and binding on secular courts.[71]

The third and most commonly used method of incorporating religious bodies is incorporation under state statutes governing nonprofit corporations. Structured like business corporations, the nonprofit corporation is governed by the congregation, which forms the voting membership of the corporation. The polity of congregational churches is best suited to this form of incorporation, whereas hierarchical polity organizations may find trustee or special charter forms of incorporation more adaptable to their needs.[72]

Denominations such as the Catholic church that place leadership and power ultimately in one individual, however, may choose a fourth form of incorporation, the corporation

---

[71]80 U.S. (13 Wall.) 679, 731 (1872).

[72]Morgan, *supra* n.69, 16 Val. U.L. Rev. at 152.

sole, a corporation composed of one person who has all the powers necessary to carry on the affairs of the corporation. Although civil authorities at first disapproved of this corporate form, the statutory reflection of this polity of episcopally structured churches is now widely accepted.[73]

Today most states have "a corporation aggregate"[74] or membership corporation structure, based on the Model Nonprofit Corporation Act.[75] The members of a church are the corporate "shareholders," and the trustees become the officers. This form is most suitable to congregational churches whose polity is democratic and thus more in conformity with the corporate pattern, but it must be adapted for churches with episcopal or other structures. For example, in hierarchical denominations the trustees may be the bishops, vicars, pastors, or elders. The decision-making processes of those denominations, however, are not necessarily democratic. Some states have separate statutes for individual denominations, while others offer more general provisions to meet the needs of different ecclesiastical bodies.[76] Legislation for incorporating a religious body ought simply to present an enabling framework that would allow the church authorities to determine the use and control of church property. Nevertheless, some statutes have mandated that church property be used according to the denomination's rules and requirements, and others have insisted that a congregation may secede from a hierarchical church only by consent of two-thirds of the congregation.[77] The California legislature, cognizant of the diversity

---

[73]*Id.* at 153.

[74]Note, *Judicial Intervention, supra* n.42, 75 Harv. L. Rev. at 1178.

[75]Morgan, *supra* n.69, 16 Val. U.L. Rev. at 152.

[76]Note, *Judicial Intervention, supra* n.42, 75 Harv. L. Rev. at 1178.

[77]*Id.* at 1177. Alabama and Mississippi are two states that have statutes requiring a two-thirds majority for secession.

of nonprofit organizations, established in its new Nonprofit Corporation Code three separate types of corporations: the mutual benefit corporation, the public benefit corporation, and the religious corporation.[78]

Even when many different corporate provisions are available, a denomination or church may choose not to incorporate. One reason may be that its polity simply is not adaptable to such a structure. Another is that a corporate statute may not sufficiently take into account the religious quality of the organization—the very quality that sets the denomination apart from other nonprofit organizations, in terms of constitutional protections, governmental regulation, and other public-policy considerations.

Several recent California court cases illustrate the difficulties that churches have encountered, either by being incorporated or unincorporated. *Samoan Congregational Christian Church v. Samoan Congregational Church of Oceanside*[79] involved a dispute between a local church and the parent denomination. When the Oceanside Church, a nonprofit religious corporation, dismissed its minister and appointed another, the unincorporated denomination disapproved. It insisted both on the denominational control of appointing a pastor, and on its right to the local church's assets because of a trust that impressed the property for the benefit of the general church. The trial court determined that the Oceanside Church assets were not impressed with a trust; the court of appeal affirmed. It examined the denominational polity and found the highest ecclesiastical authority to rest with the Mother Church in Samoa, and the highest authority in the United States to be the general assembly of the district. However, because there was

---

[78]Cal. Corp. Code §§ 5110-6910, 7110-8910, 9110-9690 (West. Supp. 1982).

[79]66 Cal. App. 3d 69, 135 Cal. Rptr. 793 (1977).

not a written constitution or other documents explaining the organizational structure, (oral testimony was instead given by two members of the ruling committee of elders) the court relied heavily on the language of the local church's corporate documents. Citing *Watson* and its progeny, the court refused to probe the sources of authority within the denomination because it felt constitutionally prohibited from doing so. It did, however, examine the corporate articles of Oceanside Church and determined that they expressed no intent to create a trust, implied or express, on behalf of the entire denomination. The polity of the church vested control of church assets with the board of directors and ownership of the property with the church corporation as a body governed by its members. Neither loyalty to the parent church organization nor obligation of trust with respect to the church assets was found as evidence to support the denomination's claims.

In a companion case, *Fuimaono v. Samoan Congregational Church of Oceanside*,[80] the church corporation was forced into dissolution. The plaintiffs were the discharged minister and forty percent of the church congregation who, along with the parent denomination, refused to acknowledge the validity of the minister's dismissal. The court declared that, because the minority faction met the statutory criteria required for a filing of dissolution, the court was required to decree that dissolution. Furthermore, because under the California laws of charitable trust the church's assets were impressed with a charitable trust and could not be distributed for private benefit, the state attorney general was charged with the duty of overseeing the proper distribution of the church's assets. *Fuimaono* underscores the fact that a court may rely on written declarations above all, and for this reason an unincorporated denomination might be at a distinct disadvantage without documents to submit as evidence of its polity. Moreover, a

---

[80]66 Cal. App. 3d 80, 135 Cal. Rptr. 799 (1977).

court may hold fast to the language of the written documents, whether or not they in fact reflect the church's intention. Although Lord Eldon's Rule of implied trust is gone, courts will enforce an express trust found in church documents. And the assets of a California religious nonprofit corporation "are deemed to be impressed with a charitable trust deriving from the express declaration of corporate purpose."[81] It is therefore important that the language of corporate purpose, and indeed of all corporate documents of a church or denomination, be drafted carefully. The terms must be clear enough to reflect the religious body's values and goals, and broad enough to allow flexibility for future changes in church doctrine or purpose.[82]

When the corporate purpose is narrowly expressed, the later intent of a religious corporation may be defeated. For example, in *Queen of Angels Hospital v. Younger*,[83] a church-operated nonprofit hospital had stated that its corporate purpose was the operation of a hospital. Later, when the hospital directors decided to establish medical clinics with money received from leasing the hospital, the court refused to approve the proposal, holding the new plan was contrary to the express purpose found in the articles of incorporation.

> . . . [W]hatever else Queen of Angels Hospital Corporation may do under its articles of incorporation, it is intended to and did operate a hospital and cannot, consistent with the trust imposed upon it, abandon the operation of the hospital business in favor of clinics.[84]

---

[81]*Samoan Congregational Church, supra* n.79, 66 Cal. App. 3d at 793.

[82]*See* Morgan, *supra*, n.69, 16 Val. U.L. Rev. at 154-56.

[83]66 Cal. App. 3d 359, 136 Cal. Rptr. 366 (1977).

[84]*Id*. at 368. 136 Cal. Rptr. at 41.

5. AGENCY IN THE NONPROFIT SECTOR

Agency encompasses those relationships for which courts will generally impose vicarious liability. The requisite characteristics of an agency that give rise to vicarious liability—consent by the principal and agent for (1) the agent to act on behalf of the principal and (2) primarily for the principal's benefit (3) with the right of the principal to control the conduct of the agent relative to the undertaking, or (4) a representation of agency and reliance thereon (these characteristics to be referred to, for brevity, as "behalf," "benefit," "control," and "reliance")[85]—are not uncomplicated rules but represent complex and shifting notions about moral and economic responsibility.[86] They raise unique problems when applied in the nonprofit context. While the application of agency concepts would not differ in the profit and nonprofit contexts when the relationships remain the same (for example, employer-employee), there are unique nonprofit relationships to which their application raises distinctive issues.

Perhaps the most important justification offered for the once-ubiquitous doctrine of charitable immunity is the altruistic nature of the activities of charities and inappropriateness of imposing liability on an organization that receives no benefit from its works.[87] The contemporary shift in attitudes toward charitable immunity has been accompanied by a cor-

---

[85] *See generally* Restatement (Second) of Agency (1957) §§ 1, 8, and §§ 12, 12, and 14 specifically for those elements of behalf, benefit, and control.

[86] *See* Morris, *Enterprise Liability and the Actuarial Process—The Insignificance of Foresight*, 70 Yale L.J. 554 (1961), for a glimpse into the variety and complexity of views.

[87] *See* Restatement (Second) of Torts § 895E comment c (1965); G.G. & G.T. Bogert, *Handbook of the Law of Trusts* 469 (5th ed. 1973).

responding shift in attitudes about the nature of charitable activities; not that they are held less worthy but that they constitute what is regularly described as the "business" of charity,[88] an organizational end—that is, benefit—to be served, the costs of which are to be the responsibility of the organization.

This contemporary view of charitable activities, however, is susceptible to an overly broad, and perhaps overly cynical, interpretation of who and what serve the "business" of charity. A church, for example, may be liable for negligence of its employees, yet it does not necessarily follow that members of its congregation are to be viewed as working on behalf or for the benefit of the church whenever they engage in good works urged upon them by church doctrine. Nor is it clear that it would make a difference, in terms of benefit to the church, if the work were done in the name of the church in response to an aspirational command thereof. Does a Boy Scout in uniform, by assisting an elderly person across the street, benefit the Boy Scouts of America? Is his action on behalf of the scout organization? There are obvious differences, it would seem, between serving an organization and serving that organization's ideals—between accomplishing duties assigned by an organization and pursuing its members' common interests or shared aspirations.

The doctrine of charitable immunity may have reflected, in part, this difficulty with the agency concept of benefit in the

---

[88]The court in *Barr*, 90 Cal. App. 3d at 271-72, 153 Cal. Rptr. at 331, described the operation of the retirement homes by the church agency as not only fulfilling "spiritual concerns" but also as "commercial activities" requiring "primarily business decisions." Statutes permitting unincorporated associations to sue and be sued often describe such an association as two or more persons transacting business under a common name. In such instances, "business" has been defined broadly to encompass nonprofit activities. *See* Comment, *Liability of Members and Officers of Nonprofit Unincorporated Association for Contracts and Torts*, 42 Calif. L. Rev. 812 (1954).

context of charity just as the income tax exemption for non-profit organizations reflects, in part, a difficulty with the concept of income in many nonprofit contexts.[89] The demise of charitable immunity, of course, settles the issue of benefit to the organization whenever an action, however altruistic, is carried out on its behalf and under its control. The elimination of charitable immunity does not resolve, however, the question of what activities are to be considered those of the organization;[90] that is to say, what actions are attributable to the organization in that they are done on its behalf and primarily for its benefit?

Activities by officers and employees and by related organizations in the profit sector do not ordinarily present problems as to on whose behalf or benefit they are taken. The status of the relationship or the scope of the employment generally resolves that issue.[91] Activities by members or affiliates of nonprofit organizations, can, however, be ambiguous because neither the members' affiliates' status, nor the scope of accepted or anticipated membership activity, is determinative. In organizations formed because of shared beliefs or ideals

---

[89]*See* Bittker & Rahdert, *The Exemption of Nonprofit Organizations from Federal Income Taxation*, 85 Yale L.J. 299 (1976).

[90]Difficulties have also been encountered with the abolition of parental and governmental immunity. For example, with parental immunity abolished, there remained the problem of incorporating parental responsibilities into the standards of care. One approach was to provide for exceptions to the abolition of parental immunity, another was to take into account the parent-child relationship in determining what an ordinarily reasonable and prudent person would do. *See Anderson v. Stream*, 295 N.W.2d 595 (Minn.1980), for a discussion of both approaches.

[91]An employee acting within the scope of his or her employment is, by definition, acting on behalf of, and for the benefit of, the employer. This is also true of a department or division of a larger organization. A subsidiary corporation is acting on behalf of the parent corporation without a showing of agency beyond the parent-subsidiary relationship.

(religious, political, and ideological groups), acts by members or affiliates constituting an expression of those beliefs and ideals are not necessarily done on behalf of and primarily for the benefit of the organization. Members and affiliates of a nonprofit organization engage in many activities, under the sponsorship of the organization or directly as a consequence of their relationship, that do not correspond to those undertaken by an agent or employee. They resemble instead those activities normally carried on by a customer, a principal, or just an interested bystander. Whether these activities should be adjudged to be on behalf of the organization and for its benefit cannot be measured by relational labels or a "scope of membership" test. Neither aegis nor affiliation in the nonprofit sector is able to provide ready answers.

Doctrinal control is exercised by many nonprofit organizations over the ideas or beliefs of participants. Irrelevant or secondary to profit organizations, doctrinal control may be fundamental to religious, political, and social organizations. Indeed, doctrinal homogeneity may constitute the only common purpose and "control" over the participants in many nonprofit groups.

Doctrine can directly and specifically bear upon actions taken on behalf of the organization. It might, for example, impose on members a requirement of obedience to the organization's leaders or mandate certain activities. The exercise of doctrinal control, therefore, is not necessarily irrelevant to questions of agency or vicarious liability.

Doctrinal control aside, authority and the right to control are often ambiguous and multidirectional in nonprofit groups. Confusion and jurisdictional overlap are common—a circumstance not too surprising when the participants have no economic stake in how the lines of authority run. Moreover, authority and control, rather than being fixed, may shift with time, circumstances, and personalities. In contrast, prerogatives and lines of authority in profit organizations tend to be definite and distinct. The extent of authority of a partner, shareholder, or affiliate is rarely vague.

These circumstances should caution against naive categorization or facile analogies between organizational complexes in the profit and nonprofit sectors. One should be alert to the numerous structures and hierarchies that may be found in nonprofit organizations, and the possibility of multiple hierarchies within a single organization. One must distinguish between doctrinal control and control exercised over organizational activities. The U.S. Supreme Court's division of church organizations into the two categories of hierarchical and congregational[92] is, in many respects, simplistic, even for the relatively limited purpose of resolving intrachurch property disputes. Yet the court in *Barr* employed this limited categorization to mold Methodists into a hierarchical church[93] and thereby imply an agency relationship between the denomination and its affiliates.

6. TRADE NAMES
IN THE NONPROFIT SECTOR

Recent decisions regarding the liability of commercial franchisors and trademark licensors for the actions of their franchises or licensees[94] are doubly instructive for our subject. The novelty, by and large, of the litigation results in decisions reflecting contemporary judicial attitudes toward ascending liability between related, albeit profit, organizations. Addi-

---

[92]*See* J. Nowak, R. Rotunda, and J. Young, *Constitutional Law*, ch. 19 § IV C (2d ed. 1983).

[93]*Barr*, 90 Cal. App. 3d 270, 153 Cal. Rptr. 330.

[94]*See* cases collected in Borchard & Ehrilich, *Franchisor Tort Liability: Minimizing the Potential Liability of a Franchisor for a Franchisee's Torts*, 69 Trademark Rep. 109 (1979); Note, *Tort Liability of Trademark Licensors*, 55 Ia. L. Rev. 693 (1970).

tionally, the organizational relationships tend, more than traditional business affiliations, to be closer to those of many nonprofit complexes.[95] Again, however, profit/nonprofit analogies are not complete.

The significance of trade names and practices can differ markedly in the nonprofit context. Many nonprofit organizations will, for valid reasons, not wish to control or protect a word or phrase in their names or organizational practices with which they are identified even though their use by another organization might cause some persons to believe that the two organizations are affiliated or that they are part of a larger whole. To control the name might, for example, require or imply unwanted authority. Thus, one Baptist church or convention will not seek to enjoin another church or organization from using the term *Baptist* since it seeks no proprietary interest in the term. Yet *Baptist* may acquire a secondary meaning,[96] partially out of ignorance and partially out of analogy to hierarchical churches, so that in the public mind two separate Baptist organizations are identified as one.

Here we find a situation quite the converse of the profit sector in which organizations ordinarily desire the establishment of a secondary meaning for a descriptive or generic term in their names in order to control or profit from its use by others. Licensing the use of a trade name to another organization may set the stage for an attendant responsibility to third parties. Indeed, the use of trade names and practices by licensees or franchises in commercial endeavors has, on occasion, given

---

[95]*See* the categorization of franchise relationships in Comment, *Theories of Liability for Retail Franchisors: A Theme and Four Variations*, 39 Md. L. Rev. 264 (1979).

[96]Secondary meaning is said to arise when a descriptive name has come to mean, in the mind of the public, the mark of a particular manufacturer. McClure, *Trademarks and Unfair Competition: A Critical History of Legal Thought*, 69 Trademark Rep. 305, 320 (1979).

rise to ascending liability.[97] Terms used in nonprofit organizations having the appearance of trade names, however, may or may not be controlled by that organization[98] or licensed to others for profit. It should not be presumed that they are. The *Chellew* case, described in chapter 5, provides an excellent example of the problems associated with shared use of denominational names by religious organizations.

---

[97]*Kasel v. Remington Arms Co.*, 24 Cal. App. 3d 711, 101 Cal. Rptr. 314 (1972), and *Gizzi v. Texaco, Inc.*, 437 F.2d 308 (3d Cir. 1971) are two of the leading cases. For others, *see* Comment, *Theories of Liability for Retail Franchisors: A Theme and Four Variations*, 39 Md. L. Rev. 264 (1979).

[98]Nonprofit organizations may, if they wish, control their names providing they have met the usual requirements. *See* Annot., 37 A.L.R. 3d 277 (1971); Kahoe, *Nonprofit Corporations' Names*, 21 Clev. St. L. Rev. 114 (1972).

II

CONSTITUTIONAL ISSUES

In 1913 a noted English theologian and political theorist, John Neville Figgis, asked rhetorically "whether, politically speaking, there is such an entity as a church; and what, if so, is the least that it can claim without committing corporate suicide."[1] Later in his lectures on *Churches in the Modern State*, Figgis answered his own question.

> It is, in a word, a real life and personality which those bodies (churches) are forced to claim, which we believe they possess by the nature of the case, and not by the arbitrary grant of the sovereign.[2]

---

[1] J. Figgis, *Churches in the Modern State* 4 (1913).

[2] *Id.* at 42.

Although it is vital that churches and religious bodies be recognized as legal entities, it does not follow that their organizational structures should be determined by the government contrary to their self-understanding. If, for example, Congress were to limit the availability of tax-exempt status under section 501(c)(3) of the Internal Revenue Code to Christian churches and thus exclude synagogues, mosques, and other forms of religious organizations, that act would clearly be an impermissible preference of one religion over another; it would violate the establishment clause of the First Amendment. If Congress were to specify further that some governmental benefit was available only to religious groups organized democratically on a local, congregational model, without any hierarchical structure of authority, such a legislative scheme would also violate the establishment clause. It would be equally impermissible for the attorney general of a state to restructure a congregational church into a hierarchical one by unilaterally altering the church's charter. It should not be any less impermissible for the judicial branch of government to do what the legislative and executive branches are proscribed from doing. The California Court of Appeals in the *Barr* case raised afresh a series of constitutional questions concerning the appropriate role of secular courts in adjudication of disputes arising within a religious group and concerning the nature of the protections afforded religious groups under both religion clauses of the First Amendment.

1. THE *BARR* COURTS
AND THE DEFINITION OF A CHURCH

It is difficult to categorize certain religious movements precisely. For example, although the fringe groups to whom John and Charles Wesley preached in the eighteenth century may not be identical with present Methodist congregations, at least these congregations preserve the Wesleyan heritage and tradition more faithfully than do any other religious groups. If the institutional structure of the contemporary United Methodist Church is more complicated than was the structure John Wesley was familiar with, it is because of organic developments over time within Methodism. And if United Methodists are more aptly described today as a church rather than as a sect, that, too, is for Methodists to decide. At various points in the life of any institution it may become necessary for it to reconsider its organizational structure and to give it more precise form. But such consideration and definition is better left to members of the institution than to outsiders. In our constitutional order the government is perhaps the least qualified of outsiders to engage in defining the organization of a religious body. The wisdom of this principle was illustrated by the conflicting definitions of the United Methodist Church set forth by the trial and appellate courts in *Barr*.

Referring both to the *Book of Discipline* of the UMC and to case law, the court categorized the denomination as hierarchical and described its various operating levels. As parts of the whole church, local churches were "subject to the higher authority of the organization and its laws and regulations."[3] Although there was no chief operating officer for the denomination, there were clearly defined levels of responsibility, from the local church to the General Conference. The court identified the Council of Bishops as the body that functions as the Board of Directors of the UMC, and the GCFA as the authorized agent in legal and financial matters for its principal, the church. The court suggested that the church's independent identity could also be verified from the UMC's appearance as a principal in other litigation and as a named insured on a contract. The court concluded that because the ecclesiastical judicial system of UMC does not provide any

---

[3]*Carnes v. Smith*, 236 Ga. 30, 222 S.E.2d 322, *cert. denied*, 429 U.S. 868, *cited in Barr*, 90 Cal. App. 3d at 268, 153 Cal. Rptr. at 328.

methods of redress for plaintiffs, the use of the secular courts as a method of dispute resolution cannot be foreclosed.[4] That description of the United Methodist Church made by the California Court of Appeal starkly contrasts with the trial court's description.

> The "United Methodist Church" is an international religious denomination consisting of over 10,000,000 persons who worship in some 43,000 churches and missions throughout the world. The "United Methodist Church" is a "connectional" structure maintained through a chain and series of periodic conferences. It has never been incorporated.[5]

Throughout the litigation the attorneys for the defendants argued that the denomination itself could not be made a party to the suit. The main elements of this argument were that the structure of the UMC is not unified or quasi-corporate and that it has no central administration and no body or individual who could speak, or indeed is allowed to speak, for the denomination in a suit. The respondents insisted that in a dispute of a secular character a court may make its own findings concerning the jural status of a religious organization and may draw its own conclusions, even if "contrary to the assertions of the religious organization's own witnesses."[6]

In the papers filed with the United States Supreme Court the denomination asserted that there were two issues that had to be kept separate: the original class-action suit involving a contractual claim, and the primary religious issue—the right of a court to interpret a church's polity and to recategorize the denomination as an unincorporated association. It insisted

---

[4]*Barr*, 90 Cal. App. 3d at 275, 153 Cal. Rptr, at 333.

[5]*Id*. at 262, n.2, 153 Cal. Rptr, at 324-25, n.2.

[6]Respondents' Brief in Opposition at 13, *Barr v. United Methodist Church*, No. 79-245 (U.S. 1979).

that the court of appeal offended the establishment clause by rejecting the denomination's expert ecclesiastical testimony and recasting the church's self-understanding according to an alien organizational structure.

The court of appeal did not separate the two issues. It agreed with the plaintiffs that the court may determine a denomination's jural status, in a suit of a secular nature, by looking at that church's structure. The court thus raised the question: who should define a church or denomination in a court of law?

The autonomy of religious groups is, of course, central to the guarantees of religious freedom in the First Amendment. For more than one hundred years, American courts have deferred to the decisions of religious bodies on ecclesiastical matters. In *Watson v. Jones*[7] the Supreme Court drew a broad line of demarcation, based on the common law of the time, but subsequently constitutionalized by the Supreme Court[8] to separate the courts' jurisdiction from the church's.

> When a civil right depends upon an ecclesiastical matter, it is the civil court and not the ecclesiastical which is to decide. But the civil tribunal tries the civil right, and no more, taking the ecclesiastical decisions out of which the civil right arises as it finds them.[9]

At the core of the First Amendment is a commitment described by Justice Miller in *Watson* more than a hundred years ago: "The law knows no heresy, and is committed to the sup-

---

[7]80 U.S. (13 Wall.) 679 (1872).

[8]*See, e.g., Presbyterian Church in the United States v. Mary Elizabeth Blue Hull Memorial Presbyterian Church*, 393 U.S. 440 (1969) (hereinafter referred to as *Blue Hull*).

[9]*Watson*, 80 U.S. at 731 (Citations omitted).

port of no dogma, the establishment of no sect."[10] Professor Tribe has described this proposition as a bedrock constitutional axiom.[11] Even though *Watson* was a diversity case in which the Supreme Court applied federal common law,[12] Justice Brennan could write nearly a century after *Watson* that the principle of noninvolvement of secular courts in intrachurch disputes had a "clear constitutional ring."[13] For Tribe the central point of *Watson* is that governmental institutions must not become entangled in religious controversies, nor "attempt to discover religious error by legal process, [n]or to promulgate religious truth by legal decree."[14]

Although a considerable degree of separation between church and state has helped to guarantee freedom in our country, some contacts between church and state are necessary and inevitable. As Professor Tribe puts it, the notion of accommodation recognizes that

> there are necessary relationships between government and religion; that government cannot be indifferent to religion in American life; and that, far from being hostile or even truly indifferent, it may, and sometimes must, accommodate its institutions and programs to the religious interests of the people.[15]

Tribe's view is correct not simply as practical political wisdom,

---

[10]*Id.* at 728.

[11]L. Tribe, *American Constitutional Law* 871 (1978).

[12]The case was decided before the Fourteenth Amendment was deemed to make the guarantees of the First Amendment applicable to the states, and so it was decided on nonconstitutional grounds.

[13]*Blue Hull*, 393 U.S. at 446.

[14]Tribe, *supra* n.11, at 871.

[15]Tribe, *supra* n.11, at 822.

but as a reflection of the commitment of most religious groups to mission or service in the world beyond the doors of the church, synagogue, or mosque. Religious bodies committed to some form of mission to the world are bound to affect the civil order in a variety of ways.

The *Barr* court acknowledged the charitable character of the mission of the United Methodist Church. Without distinguishing the activities of the separately incorporated Pacific Homes, however, the court stated that the very involvement of the church in society that the court commended constituted sufficient grounds for the courts' jurisdiction over the entire denomination:

> UMC, in fulfilling its commitment to society, has elected to involve itself in worldly activities by participating in many socially valuable projects. It has enjoyed the benefits, both economic and spiritual, of those projects. It has even on occasion filed suit for the protection of its interests. It must now, as part of its involvement in society, be amenable to suit.[16]

The working partnership between church and state in the realm of social welfare may thus involve some tension. The balance must be struck somewhere between excessive regulation and total noninterference. Within this intermediate zone, the government may make reasonable accommodations to legitimate interests of religious groups without thereby appearing to prefer or to establish a religion.[17] This

---

[16]*Barr*, 90 Cal. App. 3d at 272, 153 Cal. Rptr. at 331.

[17]In another area, the Supreme Court has expressly acknowledged the power of Congress to go beyond noninterference by accommodating what it feels is a legitimate free exercise interest, and the Court has deferred to that congressional protection of religious beliefs, even though that protection shows a preference for a particular religious belief, thereby violating the nonestablishment principle. *Compare Welsh v. United States*, 398 U.S. 333 (1970) *with Gilette v. United States*, 401 U.S. 437 (1971).

accommodationist perspective was not adopted by the court of appeals in *Barr*, which suggested that it had to treat the United Methodist Church as it would any other association or corporation in order to avoid the appearance of giving preference to a religious body.[18] In its concern to avoid the semblance of a preference for religion, the *Barr* court overlooked the practical wisdom of Aristotle's notion that it is unjust to treat unequals equally, for to treat the United Methodist Church as though it were General Motors is to miss an important distinction between a profit corporation and a religious association that is nonprofit.

2. THE NONESTABLISHMENT PRINCIPLE

The First Amendment originally functioned as a restraint on the federal government rather than on the states. But in this century the Court began the gradual process of selectively incorporating various provisions of the Bill of Rights into the Fourteenth Amendment as an aspect of the "ordered concept of liberty" protected by the due process clause.[19]

In 1940 the Court ruled in *Cantwell v. Connecticut*[20] that the free exercise of religion was part of the fundamental concept of liberty protected by the Fourteenth Amendment; Justice Roberts added a dictum in his opinion to the effect that the Fourteenth Amendment also prohibited state legislatures

---

[18]*Barr*, 90 Cal. App. 3d at 275, 153 Cal. Rptr. at 333, *citing Abington School District v. Schempp*, 374 U.S. 203 (1963).

[19]*See, e.g., Twining v. New Jersey*, 211 U.S. 78 (1908); *Near v. Minnesota*, 283 U.S. 697 (1931); *Palko v. Connecticut*, 302 U.S. 319 (1937); *Adamson v. California*, 332 U.S. 46 (1947); *Duncan v. Louisiana*, 391 U.S. 145 (1968).

[20]310 U.S. 296 (1940).

from enacting laws respecting the establishment of religion. The Court relied on this view in *McCollum v. Board of Education*[21] to strike down under the establishment clause a state law allowing voluntary released-time religious instruction of public school students on public property. Since *McCollum*, the Court has taken for granted that it has textual authority in the Fourteenth and First Amendments to invalidate state legislation or official practices involving religious instruction in public schools[22] and public assistance to religiously affiliated nonpublic schools and students attending them.[23]

Like other aspects of First Amendment law such as the law of libel, judicial interpretations of the establishment clause since 1940 have not yielded a very clear or coherent body of constitutional doctrine.

Although Supreme Court justices and constitutional scholars alike have been critical of the Supreme Court's establishment clause jurisprudence, Justice Black reflected a clear consensus when he wrote in *Everson v. Board of Education*[24] that the gist of the clause was that "religious liberty [could] be secured best under a *neutral* government, one which neither

---

[21]333 U.S. 203 (1948).

[22]*See, e.g., Engel v. Vitale*, 370 U.S. 421 (1962); *Abington School District v. Schempp*, 374 U.S. 203 (1963); *but see Widmar v. Vincent*, 454 U.S. 263 (1981).

[23]*See, e.g., Lemon v. Kurtzman*, 403 U.S. 602 (1971); *Committee for Public Education and Religious Liberty v. Nyquist*, 413 U.S. 756 (1973); *Meek v. Pittenger*, 421 U.S. 349 (1975), and *Wolman v. Walter*, 433 U.S. 229 (1977); *but see Tilton v. Richardson*, 403 U.S. 672 (1971), *Hunt v. McNair*, 413 U.S. 736 (1976); and *Committee for Public Education and Religious Liberty v. Regan*, 446 U.S. 646 (1980).

[24]330 U.S. 1 (1947).

supports nor assists religion."[25] In *Zorach v. Clauson*,[26] however, Justice Douglas moved beyond the concept of governmental neutrality, noting that the First Amendment does not require "callous indifference to religious groups,"[27] but should be held to embrace reasonable accommodations to the spiritual and religious needs of the people. In *Engel v. Vitale*,[28] the Court invalidated the public recital of the state-composed Regents' prayer on the grounds that the practices violated governmental neutrality and created a union of government and religion tending to destroy government and degrade religion. In *Board of Education v. Allen*[29] the Court sustained a New York statute authorizing the loan of secular textbooks to children attending nonpublic schools because it viewed the statute as "completely neutral with regard to religion."[30] Chief Justice Burger stretched the meaning of neutrality when he suggested in *Walz v. Tax Commission*[31] that neutrality should be "benevolent," permitting "religious exercise to exist without sponsorship and without interference"[32] since for Burger, the purpose of

---

[25]*Id*. (emphasis supplied). Black went beyond the historical evidence when he asserted: "The 'establishment of religion' clause . . . means at least this: Neither a state nor the Federal Government . . . can pass laws which *aid . . . all* religions." *Id*. at 15 (emphasis supplied). Both the state and federal governments did just that. *See, e.g.*, R. Cord, *Separation of Church and State: Historical Fact and Current Fiction* (1982).

[26]343 U.S. 306 (1952).

[27]*Id*. at 314.

[28]370 U.S. 421 (1962).

[29]392 U.S. 236 (1968).

[30]*Id*. at 241.

[31]397 U.S. 664 (1970).

[32]*Id*. at 669.

the establishment clause is "to insure that no religion be sponsored or favored, none commanded and none inhibited."[33]

The Court's formulation of the concept of governmental neutrality as central to the nonestablishment principle has thus traversed a meandering path. If the Court's utterances on governmental neutrality in religious matters have not yielded analytical precision or clarity,[34] at least they support the conclusion that the government ought not change the self-understanding of religious bodies nor interfere with their internal structure.[35]

Perhaps it was dissatisfaction with the nebulousness of the Court's treatment of the concept of governmental neutrality that prompted the Court to specify standards for adjudicating claims arising under the establishment clause. In *Lemon v. Kurtzman*[36] the Court announced that it would henceforth scrutinize legislation challenged under the establishment clause by applying a tripartite test "developed by the Court over many years."

---

[33]*Id.*

[34]For a creative attempt to elevate the Court's teaching on neutrality to the level of a principle, *see* Kurland, *Of Church and State and the Supreme Court*, 29 U. Chi. L. Rev. 1 (1961). For a critique of Kurland's position as undermining protections secured under the free exercise clause, *see e.g.*, Merel, *The Protection of Individual Choice: A Consistent Understanding of Religion Under the First Amendment*, 45 U. Chi. L. Rev. 805 (1978).

[35]"[I]f properly limited, the concept [of neutrality] expresses at least a minimum requirement of the first amendment—that the government not take sides on religious questions, favoring some answers or sects over others." L. Tribe, *supra* n.11, at 867 n.12.

[36]401 U.S. 602 (1971) (invalidating state statutes authorizing purchase of services of instruction in secular subjects at religiously affiliated elementary and secondary schools in Pennsylvania and salary supplements for teachers of secular subjects at such schools in Rhode Island).

First, the statute must have a secular legislative purpose; second, its principal or primary effect must be one
that neither advances nor inhibits religion; finally, the statute must not foster an excessive government entanglement
with religion.[37]

Although statutes must have a valid secular purpose, this
requirement does not mean that a statute cannot *also* fulfill
some religious purpose.[38] Professor Tribe regards the requirement that "governmental action at least be justifiable in
secular terms" as "the most fundamental requirement in a
constitutional system designed to secure religious autonomy."[39]
He is quick to add, moreover, that the understanding of what
is "secular" must be broad: "if a purpose were to be classified
as non-secular simply because it coincided with the beliefs of
one religion or took its origin from another, virtually nothing
that government does would be acceptable; laws against mur-
der, for example, would be forbidden because they overlapped
the fifth commandment of the Mosaic decalogue."[40] Tribe
notes further, "the Court will usually find in the statutory language or elsewhere a secular purpose for the challenged law,
and will then move on to considerations of the remaining two
criteria."[41]

---

[37]*Id*. at 612-13. This tripartite formulation has recurred in subsequent
establishment clause cases. *See, e.g., Hunt v. McNair*, 413 U.S. 734, 743
(1973).

[38]*See, e.g., Bradfield v. Roberts*, 175 U.S. 291 (1899).

[39]Tribe, *supra* n.11, at 835.

[40]*Id*. "American courts have not thought the separation of church and
state to require that religion be totally oblivious to government or politics;
church and religious groups in the United States have long exerted pow-
erful political pressures on state and national legislatures, on subjects as
diverse as slavery, war, gambling, drinking, prostitution, marriage, and education." *Id*. at 866-67.

[41]*Id*. at 836.

The second criterion is that the principal and primary effect of governmental action must neither advance nor inhibit religion. The effect test has been modified at times to allow imaginable side effects to be articulated as the basis for invalidating a statute.[42] But recently, the Court has returned to a stricter formulation of the test, stating that a statute may be invalidated only if it has the "direct and immediate effect of advancing religion" and noting explicitly that a "remote and incidental effect advantageous to religious institutions" would not suffice to strike down a statute.[43] Acknowledging that governmental policies may have both secular and religious effects, Professor Tribe regards the Court's distinction between direct and indirect effects and between immediate and incidental effects as impossible and unnecessary.[44] For Tribe, the questions posed by the requirement of secular effect concern the separability of the secular impact on governmental action from the religious impact and the breadth of the class of persons benefiting from the action.[45]

The third criterion is that a challenged statute or governmental action must not foster an excessive entanglement of the government with religion. First announced in *Walz* as an aspect of the primary effect test, the excessive entanglement test was acknowledged by Chief Justice Burger to be "inescapably

---

[42]*Committee for Public Education and Religious Liberty v. Nyquist*, 413 U.S. 756 (1973).

[43]*Larkin v. Grendel's Den*, 103 S.Ct. 505, 508 (1982) *citing Nyquist*, 413 U.S. at 783.

[44]Tribe, *supra* n.11, at 840.

[45]*Id.*, commenting on *Roemer v. Board of Public Works of Maryland*, 426 U.S. 736 (1976) and *Wolman v. Walter*, 433 U.S. 229 (1977), Tribe analyzes the separability standard at 841-44. Commenting on *Nyquist, supra* n.42, and *Walz, supra* n.31, Tribe analyzes the standard relating to the breadth of the beneficiary class at 845-46.

one of degree."[46] Both taxation of religious bodies and exemption from taxation would lead to some involvement of the government with religion, but tax exemption was sustained in *Walz* on the grounds that it would result in less entanglement with religion than would taxation. In *Lemon*, Burger clarified that the kind of administrative entanglement he deemed impermissible was "comprehensive, discriminating, and continuing state surveillance"[47] of religious organizations. Tribe describes the requirement of refraining from excessive entanglement as a basic component of the nonestablishment principle because it restates the Madisonian vision of the relationship between church and state.

It should be clear that the court of appeals in *Barr* erred when it suggested that the nonestablishment principle would be offended by a policy that treated religious groups differently than profit corporations, or even—for that matter—than other nonprofit corporations. First, the valid, secular purpose underlying such a policy is grounded in the secular constitutional value of autonomy of religious groups. At the very least, this autonomy requires that all governmental officials, including judges, refrain from redefining a church's structure in a manner inconsistent with the church's self-understanding. Second, the primary or prinicipal effect of such a policy would not be to advance any particular religious perspective. To the contrary, the *Barr* court offended against the primary effect test by inhibiting the ability of the United Methodist Church to structure itself as it chooses. Third, the prohibition of excessive entanglement likewise requires an opposite result from that reached by the *Barr* court. Excessive entanglement can take the form not simply of comprehensive monitoring of public funds given to a religious body, but of inappropriate

---

[46]*Walz*, 397 U.S. at 674.

[47]*Lemon*, 403 U.S. at 619.

governmental involvement in the internal decision making of a religious group. In Professor Tribe's view, the latter form of entanglement most subverts the value of religious autonomy because it "involves government not only in the *apparatus* of religion but in its very *spirit*—in its decisions on core matters of belief and ritual."[48]

3. THE FREE EXERCISE PRINCIPLE

The prohibition against excessive entanglement of the government with religion has been articulated in establishment-clause cases, but it implicates the free exercise of religion as well. Because the decision of the *Barr* court opens the door to further judicial intermeddling in the internal matters of the faith and polity of religious groups, some analysis of the free exercise principle related to the entanglement concern is in order.

First, the civil liberty of religious freedom is enjoyed not only by isolated individuals who maintain religious beliefs and practices on their own, but by churches or religious societies that maintain such beliefs and practices in consort. The value of associational freedom is not specified in so many words in the Bill of Rights, but it has been recognized by the Supreme Court as a corollary of the rights explicitly protected by the First Amendment. This view was announced first in *NAACP v. Alabama ex rel. Patterson*.[49] The theory that has developed since that case is that the First Amendment protects not only an individual's right to freedom of speech or assembly or right to petition the government for redress of grievance, but also con-

---

[48]Tribe, *supra* n.11, at 870, *citing Watson v. Jones* 80 U.S. (13 Wall.) 679, 729 (1872): "It would lead to the total subversion of religious bodies if anyone aggrieved by one of their decisions could appeal to the secular courts and have them reversed."

[49]357 U.S. 449 (1958); *see* Tribe, *supra* n.11, at 700-10.

certed activity by a group to exercise these freedoms. Similarly, rights of religious freedom have an associational ring to them.

The central message that emerges from Supreme Court decisions articulating a right to freedom of association is that this freedom insulates private groups from unreasonable government interference in their internal affairs. Among the voluntary associations the Court has protected in this are labor organizations,[50] political parties,[51] civil rights groups,[52] and the management of banks and corporations.[53] By the same token, religious groups merit similar protection.[54]

Second, the core value of free exercise of religion is that the government may not unduly interfere with the beliefs of a religious body, including its traditions concerning its polity or self-governance. At minimum this value means that the government may not impose a belief against the choice of an individual or a group. This teaching was enunciated clearly in the second flag-salute case, *West Virginia State Board of Education v. Barnette*,[55] in which Justice Roberts stated: "If there is any fixed star in our constitutional constellation, it is that no official, high or petty, can prescribe what shall be orthodox in politics, nationalism, religion, or other matters of opinion or

---

[50]*See, e.g., United Transportation Union v. Michigan*, 401 U.S. 576 (1971).

[51]*See, e.g., Buckley v. Valeo*, 424 U.S. 1 (1976).

[52]*See, e.g., Bates v. City of Little Rock*, 361 U.S. 516 (1960).

[53]*See, e.g., First National Bank of Boston v. Bellotti*, 435 U.S. 765 (1978).

[54]*See, e.g., Kedroff v. St. Nicholas Cathedral*, 344 U.S. 94 (1952); *see also Serbian Orthodox Diocese v. Milivojevich*, 426 U.S. 696 (1976).

[55]319 U.S. 624 (1943) (invalidating state requirement that public school children salute the flag).

force citizens to confess by work or act their faith therein."[56]
The government may require a show of sincerity of religious
belief,[57] but it may not challenge or demand proof of the
truthfulness or validity of religious convictions. As Justice
Douglas observed in *United States v. Ballard,*

> Freedom of thought, which includes freedom of reli-
> gious belief, . . . embraces the right to maintain theories of
> life and of death and of the hereafter which are rank her-
> esy to followers of the orthodox faiths. . . . Men may believe
> what they cannot prove. *They may not be put to the proof of their
> religious doctrines or beliefs.* Religious experiences which are
> as real as life to some may be incomprehensible to others.
> Yet the fact that they may be beyond the ken of mortals
> does not mean that they can be made suspect before the
> law.[58]

The *Barr* court paid insufficient attention to these two core
values of the free exercise principle when it substituted its own
judgment concerning the polity of a major religious denomination for that of the denomination itself.

The difficulty courts have had in defining religion in free
exercise cases highlights the problems inherent in this judicial
definition. In two of the draft cases, for example, the Supreme
Court expanded the traditional understanding of religion. In

---

[56]*Id.* at 642. *See also Wooley v. Maynard,* 430 U.S. 705 (1977) (reversing
conviction of a Jehovah's Witness for covering a motto on an automobile
license plate deemed by the defendant to be morally, ethically, religiously,
and politically abhorrent).

[57]*See* Tribe, *supra* n.11, at 859-62. *See, e.g., Sherbert v. Verner,* 374 U.S.
398 (1963) and *Thomas v. Review Board Indiana Employment Security Division,*
450 U.S. 707 (1981).

[58]322 U.S. 78, 86-87 (1944).

United States v. Seeger,[59] the Court instructed the Congress and the Executive that they could not require belief in a Supreme Being as a component of "religious training or belief" requisite for the statutory exemption for conscientious objectors to military service. It would suffice that a conscientious objector has a sincere and meaningful belief that "occupies a place in the life of its possessor parallel to that filled by the orthodox belief in God."[60] In *Welsh v. United States*[61] the Court expanded the definition even further, allowing purely ethical convictions to be considered religious if they were felt intensely. A person could be refused conscientious objector status only if his belief "does not rest at all upon moral, ethical, or religious principle but instead rests solely upon considerations of policy, pragmatism, or expediency."[62]

After *Seeger* and *Welsh*, governmental officials are thus obliged to allow loose, functional definitions of religious beliefs. It therefore seems clear that the *Barr* court was insensitive to the thorny problem of governmental definition of religion when it insisted on a tighter definition of the organizational structure of a religious organization than was offered by the religious body at trial and accepted as correct by the trial court. A church's self-understanding, including its beliefs, expressions of worship, and operational structure should not be circumscribed or altered by governmental acts, least of all by judges bound in oath to affirm and uphold the constitutional value of free exercise of religion.

A third component of free exercise jurisprudence states that, once it has been shown that a person's or group's reli-

---

[59]380 U.S. 163 (1965).

[60]*Id*. at 166.

[61]398 U.S. 333 (1970).

[62]*Id*. at 342-43.

gious convictions have been compromised by a governmental act, that act can be sustained only if the government can show that it has been adopted to further a compelling state interest and that no other means of achieving this goal could be adopted that would be less intrusive upon religious freedom. This rule was first announced in *Sherbert v. Verner*,[63] strengthened in *Wisconsin v. Yoder*,[64] and recently reaffirmed in *Thomas v. Review Board Indiana Employment Security Dvision*.[65] *Sherbert*, *Yoder*, and *Thomas* involved conflicts between the government and individuals asserting that governmental acts deprived them of a benefit to which they were entitled. The situation presented in *Barr* was different in that it involved a conflict between governmental authority and a religious group. In this latter sort of case the values of the free exercise principle outlined above merge with the prohibition against excessive entanglement articulated in the discussion of the nonestablishment principle.

An illustration of the application of the *Sherbert-Yoder-Thomas* line of thought as well as the entanglement concern is found in *Surinach v. Pesquera de Busquets*.[66] In *Surinach* the Department of Consumer Affairs of Puerto Rico subpoenaed financial records of all Catholic elementary and secondary schools. The religious group refused to comply with the subpoena on the grounds that it constituted unwarranted governmental interference with church affairs. The appellate court sustained the church's refusal to comply, relying on *Sherbert* for its conclusion that the government had not shown that its request for the financial information would serve a compelling state interest and that there was "no less restrictive or *entan-*

---

[63]374 U.S. 398 (1963).

[64]406 U.S. 205 (1972).

[65]450 U.S. 707 (1981).

[66]602 F.2d 73 (1st Cir. 1979).

gling alternative"[67] than the sweeping subpoena that it issued to the church. The *Surinach* court observed further that in cases like this the government must be held to a standard of clear and convincing evidence "because the court is dealing with a claim which holds a preferred position and has far-reaching social consequences," and suggested that this standard "fits the requirements of close scrutiny mandated by the religion clauses of the First Amendment."[68] The *Surinach* case thus illustrates that both the nonestablishment principle and the free exercise principle suggest a different conclusion than was reached by the *Barr* court. The conjunction of these principles in *Surinach* serves, moreover, to introduce the theme of civil adjudication of intrachurch disputes, which is a judicial blend of the concern for avoiding excessive governmental entanglement with religion and the concern that religious groups retain autonomy and freedom over their own religious beliefs and polity.

4. CIVIL ADJUDICATION OF INTRACHURCH DISPUTES

Religious organizations act upon their beliefs, and their acts are bound to affect the lives of some of the members of their own congregations. As in *Barr*, these acts sometimes lead to disputes; those disputes, tinged with religious belief, are sometimes brought before civil courts for resolution. It is, of course, clear from *Watson v. Jones*[69] and *Kedroff v. St. Nicholas Cathedral*[70] that religious doctrines must be kept beyond the

---

[67]*Id.* at 79 (emphasis supplied).

[68]*Id.*

[69]80 U.S. (13 Wall.) 679 (1872).

[70]344 U.S. 94 (1952); *see also Kreshik v. St. Nicholas Cathedral*, 363 U.S. 190 (1960).

reach of civil court determinations. Secular courts are the proper forums for the adjudication of purely secular claims to property, but as Justice Miller put it in *Watson*, the ecclesiastical decisions affecting those rights must be accepted by the court "as it finds them."[71] Like the language of the religion clauses, this summary of the relationship between church and state is short, concise, and yet problematic. There will always be relations between church and state, and civil authorities will always be called upon to resolve disputes arising among members of a religious body. The problem of possible judicial interpretation of religious doctrine in such situations has been made more complex by the variety of structures found in religious organizations in our society.[72]

The American commitment to noninvolvement by the judiciary in intrachurch disputes developed at least partially in response to English common law, which freely interpreted church doctrine when it arose in legal disputes. *Attorney General v. Pearson*,[73] involved a dispute over control of the church meetinghouse by two rival groups. Lord Eldon's position was that when property was contributed to a church, there was an understanding that the donation implied support for the church's beliefs and was to be held in trust for the propagation of those beliefs. The Chancellor characterized that understanding as an implied trust in favor of the fundamental doctrines of the church. If a dispute arose subsequently over the church property, Eldon suggested that this court should award the property to the group most faithful to those doctrines and practices that were followed when the contribution was made. The court had to determine what the fundamental church

---

[71]*Watson*, 80 U.S. at 731.

[72]*See, e.g.*, Note, *Judicial Intervention in Disputes Over the Use of Church Property*, 75 Harv. L. Rev. 1142 (1962).

[73]3 Mer. 353, 36 Eng. Rep. 135 (Ch. 1817).

doctrines at the time of the donation were in order to award the property. Professor Tribe notes that this role "was consistent with a legal system that included an established church under parliamentary control."[74] Lord Eldon's implied trust theory became precedent in all English church-property dispute cases.

Throughout the early nineteenth century, American courts followed the implied trust theory, but soon realized that civil authorities were unable to decide competently matters of religious doctrine. Furthermore, courts recognized that the judicial demand that religious bodies remain faithful to past doctrines was stifling the growth and autonomy of churches.[75] Another reason for abandoning the implied trust doctrine was that it entailed a commingling of the personal and political opinions of judges with their interpretation of religious doctrine. By the 1830s various state courts began to abandon the implied trust doctrine.[76] Thus, when Justice Miller announced in *Watson*[77] that as a matter of federal common law, federal courts were not to follow the English approach of construing an implied trust, he was encapsulating a development of more than four decades in American judicial policy recognizing limits on judicial authority in the resolution of intrachurch disputes.

The *Watson* case began with a divided Kentucky church in 1866. The Walnut Street Presbyterian Church had separated into two groups that were arguing ostensibly over the use and control of the church property; the dispute, however, was ac-

---

[74]*See* Tribe, *supra* n.11, at 872.

[75]*See, e.g.*, C. Zollman, *American Church Law* at 238-39 (1933).

[76]*See, e.g.*, *Trustees of the Organ Meeting House v. Seaford*, 16 N.C. (1 Dev. Eq.) 453 (1830); *Keyser v. Stansifer*, 6 Ohio 364 (1934); *Smith v. Nelson*, 18 Vt. 202 (1846); and *Robertson v. Bullions*, 11 N.Y. 243 (1854).

[77]80 U.S. (13 Wall.) 679 (1872).

tually concerned with the church's position on slavery. The General Assembly of the Presbyterian Church had announced that no one who believed in slavery could be received into the church until he repented of that sin. One group of the Walnut Street Church was loyal to the beliefs they had always held, which had accepted slavery; the other group followed the edict of the General Assembly. The Supreme Court recognized that the case was one of division or schism in the Presbyterian Church rather than merely of use of church property.[78] Justice Miller then divided the issues concerning property rights in church disputes into three categories, suggesting that civil courts should determine those rights on the basis of the category in which it fit. First, if the property in question was held under the express terms of some instrument, to be used for a particular purpose or in support of a specific doctrine, then the court had to uphold that express trust. But when no will or deed had expressed the purpose for which the property was to be used, then that determination had to be made by the appropriate religious authority. Justice Miller's second category is the congregational type or independent church that, "so far as church government is concerned, owes no fealty or obligation to any higher authority."[79] The third category in *Watson* is the hierarchical church, one in which there is an ascending order of authority, and in which a local church must look to "superior ecclesiastical tribunals with a general and ultimate power of control."[80]

If the property is held by a congregational, self-governing organization, the body vested with ultimate decision-making power within the congregation may exercise that power in allocating the property. If the polity or method of governing the

---

[78]*Id*. at 717.

[79]*Id*. at 722.

[80]*Id*.

congregation is based on the will of the majority, for example, then the majority may control the right to use of the assets. On the other hand, if a hierarchical type of church holds the property, then the superior ecclesiastical court will hear and decide the property-right issue. The secular judicial decision must not be based on a determination concerning departure from the fundamental doctrines on which the church was established. Ecclesiastical decisions reached by the church tribunals must be accepted as final and binding on the civil courts; only the civil right may be determined by civil courts.

In 1952 the Supreme Court reaffirmed the holding in *Watson* and "implied that it was required by the free exercise and establishment clauses of the First Amendment."[81] *Kedroff v. St. Nicholas Cathedral*[82] was the first case that considered the constitutionality of government intervention in intrachurch conflicts. St. Nicholas is the Russian Orthodox Cathedral in New York City. In its hierarchical structure the highest authority of the Russian Orthodox Church is the Patriarch of Moscow. An American group attempted to separate the American branch of the orthodox churches by taking control of St. Nicholas. In 1945 a New York statute validated that schism by "declaring the American group the legitimate representative of Russian Orthodoxy and as such entitled to the property of the Russian Orthodox Church in New York."[83] The Supreme Court ruled that the statute violated the free exercise clause by preventing the legitimate hierarchy from acting upon its ecclesiastical decisions free of government interference. On remand, the New York Court of Appeals found that the Soviet branch of the Russian Orthodox Church

---

[81]Tribe, *supra* n.11, at 873.

[82]344 U.S. 94 (1952).

[83]N.Y. Laws 1945, ch. 693, as amended, N.Y. Laws 1948, ch. 711, §1 (now appearing as N.Y. Relig. Corp. Law §105).

was represented in the United States by Soviet agents who were not proper trustees and who would not uphold the original purposes for which the cathedral was established. It, therefore, reaffirmed the ownership of the cathedral by the American faction. In *Kreshik v. St. Nicholas Cathedal*,[84] the Supreme Court again reversed the lower state-court ruling. Just as the First Amendment prevented the legislature from interfering with the control of the church by the Patriarch of Moscow, so too it prohibited judicial determination of the matter.

Although *Kedroff* and *Kreshik* warned the states neither to interfere with church ecclesiastical decisions nor to interpret theological doctrines in disputes over property, they did not concern themselves with the ideas of implied trust or the departure from doctrine standard, which some states continued to use. In 1969 the Supreme Court overturned a Georgia decision based upon departure from original church doctrine. *Presbyterian Church in the United States v. Mary Elizabeth Blue Hull Memorial Presbyterian Church*[85] involved two Savannah churches that had withdrawn from the general Presbyterian Church because "certain actions of the pronouncements of the general church were violations of that organization's constitution and departure from the doctrine and practice in force at the time of affiliation."[86] Among those acts of the general church were the ordination of women; use of neo-orthodox literature; support of the removal of Bible readings in public schools; membership in the National Council of Churches of Christ; and issuance of pronouncements on Vietnam and other social and political matters. By jury verdict the trial court declared that the general church's actions indicated a substantial abandonment of the original church tenets;

---

[84]363 U.S. 190 (1960).

[85]393 U.S. 440 (1969).

[86]*Id.* at 442.

therefore the implied trust of local church property for the benefit of the general church had been terminated. Thus, the local churches retained control of the property. The Supreme Court of Georgia affirmed, but the United States Supreme Court reversed on First Amendment grounds. Justice Brennan wrote that a civil court's use of the departure-from-doctrine test in resolving church-property disputes is forbidden by the religion clauses: "[T]he First Amendment severely circumscribes the role that civil courts may play in resolving church property disputes."[87] In that narrow realm in which a judicial determination is appropriate, Brennan offered guidance both to courts and to churches.

> [T]here are neutral principles of law, developed for use in all property disputes, which can be applied without "establishing" churches to which property is awarded. But First Amendment values are plainly jeopardized when church property litigation is made to turn on the resolution by civil courts of controversies over religious doctrine and practice. . . . Hence, states, religious organizations, and individuals must structure relations involving church property so as not to require the civil courts to resolve ecclesiastical questions.[88]

The most recent Supreme Court decision concerning a dispute over church property, *Jones v. Wolf*,[89] also arose from a schism in a Presbyterian church in Georgia. When the majority of the local congregation voted to separate from the general Presbyterian denomination, the higher body in the church's hierarchical structure appointed a commission to investigate. The commission determined that the minority faction was the "true" congregation; that class of parishioners

---

[87]*Id*. at 449.

[88]*Id*.

[89]443 U.S. 595 (1979).

then sought declaratory and injunctive relief to establish its right to exclusive possession of the church. Both the Georgia trial court and Supreme Court upheld the right of the majority group to the church, and the United States Supreme Court found these determinations constitutionally sound. Justice Blackmun scrutinized the method used by the Georgia Supreme Court for resolving the church dispute by the "neutral principles of law" mentioned by Justice Brennan in the *Blue Hull* case.[90] The Georgia court would first examine all relevant documents (such as church property deeds, the corporate charter, constitution or religious tract of the denomination), searching for an indication of intention on the part of the parties to create a trust. If there were no basis in the documents for finding a trust under applicable state law, the court would award the property to the party with legal title to it. In *Jones v. Wolf*, after looking for language of trust in legal documents and the *Book of Church Order*, the court found no indication of an express trust. It therefore awarded the property to a majority of the local congregation in which the legal title was vested.[91]

The United States Supreme Court approved the Georgia court's method, holding that a state is constitutionally entitled to adopt "neutral principles of law" as a means of adjudicating a church-property dispute.[92] The Court, however, vacated the judgment of the Georgia court and remanded the case in order to clarify the basis on which the court had determined that the majority faction represented the local church. As Justice Blackmun summarized this dispute,

Petitioners earnestly submit that the question of which fac-

---

[90]Tribe, *supra*, n.11.

[91]443 U.S. 595, 601 (1979).

[92]*Id*. at 604.

tion is the true representative of the Vineville church is an ecclesiastical question that cannot be answered by a civil court. At least, it is said, it cannot be answered by a civil court in a case involving a hierarchical church, like the PCUS, where a duly appointed church commission has determined which of the two factions represents the "true congregation." Respondents, in opposition, argue in effect that the Georgia courts did no more than apply the ordinary presumption that, absent some indication to the contrary, a voluntary religious association is represented by a majority of its members.[93]

Noting that the Georgia court awarded the property to the majority faction, Blackmun observed that a "presumptive rule" of majority representation, defeasible upon a showing that the identity of the local church is to be determined by some other means, would be consistent with both the neutral-principles analysis and the First Amendment.[94]

Blackmun's opinion elicited a sharp dissent from Justice Powell, joined by the Chief Justice, Justice Stewart, and Justice White.[95] Relying on "long-established precedents" in intra-church disputes that require "a court to give effect in all cases to the decisions of the church government agreed upon by the members before the dispute arose,"[96] the dissenters insisted that a secular court should first locate the ultimate authority within a religious association, according to its rules of polity, and should follow the decision of the proper authority. Justice Powell characterized the procedure offered by the majority "under the attractive banner of neutral principles"[97] as a "new

[93]*Id.* at 610.

[94]*Id.*

[95]*Id.* at 610 (Powell, J., dissenting).

[96]*Id.* at 614.

[97]*Id.* at 614.

and complex two-stage analysis" that "inevitably will increase the involvement of civil courts in church controversies."[98] In the first stage the court looks for trust language in church documents. If the property is held in trust for the general church organization, the court grants control of the property to the denomination in the second stage; if there is no trust, the court will turn control back to the local congregation. And if the schism is within the local church itself, the court must apply the same two-step process in order to determine which faction should have the property.

The majority opinion in *Jones v. Wolf* recognized that courts must exercise special care both to examine religious documents "in purely secular terms" when looking for an intention of creating a trust, and to relinquish resolution of any ecclesiastical issues that may be present. Justice Blackmun argued unpersuasively that this approach is constitutionally sound because it is "neutral" and nonentangling.[99] To Powell's insistence that in church-property disputes civil courts are constitutionally mandated to "defer to the 'authoritative resolution of the dispute within the church itself,' " Blackmun replied that there is no First Amendment requirement of compulsory deference to religious authority.[100] Indeed, Blackmun suggested that the rule offered by Powell would draw secular courts into a "searching and therefore impermissible inquiry into church policy,"[101] while the neutral-principles ap-

---

[98]*Id.* at 611.

[99]*Id.* at 603. Justice Blackmun also refers to the mandate in *Blue Hull* that religious organizations and civil governments "structure their relationships involving church property so as not to require the civil courts to resolve ecclesiastical questions." 393 U.S. 440, 449. As this clarification is made, determining the roles of church and state will become simpler.

[100]*Id.* at 605.

[101]*Id.* at 605, *citing Serbian Eastern Orthodox Diocese v. Milivojevich,* 426 U.S. 696, 723, (1976).

proach demands no such inquiry. Blackmun quickly dismissed the claim that this approach would inhibit the free exercise of religion by religious bodies, noting that they may state freely and clearly in any of their constitutive documents the appropriate procedures to be followed in resolving church-property disputes by using language of legal trust. According to Blackmun, "the civil courts will be bound to give effect to the result indicated by the parties, provided it is embodied in some legally cognizable form."[102]

Justice Blackmun explained that the case was being remanded in order that the Georgia court might explain the basis upon which it determined that the majority represented the local church. If the court simply applied "the ordinary presumption that, absent some indication to the contrary, a voluntary religious association is represented by a majority of its members,"[103] the Supreme Court would approve that rule. It would be constitutionally sound and consistent with the neutral-principles analysis, and would remove the possibility of interference with church polity or doctrine. If, however, under Georgia law the proper means of identifying the faction representing the church involved considerations of religious doctrine and polity, then the court would be constitutionally required to defer to the denomination's determination of that church's identity.

The neutral-principles analysis of *Blue Hull* and *Jones v. Wolf*, then, may be used to resolve church-property disputes as long as there is no judicial interference in the constitutionally protected areas of religion. However, the *Jones* court was sharply divided over the validity of this approach. All the Justices recognized the validity of a general rule prohibiting civil courts from passing on questions of religious doctrine. The

---

[102]*Id.* at 606.

[103]*Id.* at 607.

majority argued that its neutral-principles approach observed that rule faithfully. Justice Powell's dissent, however, suggests that the basic underlying issue in the case was a religious one and that greater judicial deference to the proper ecclesiastical authority is therefore appropriate.

Both the majority and minority opinions in *Jones* acknowledge that a court may not delve into church polity. In several major First Amendment cases the Supreme Court has upheld the integrity of religious organizations "viewed as organic units,"[104] and has recognized their right to exercise their religion freely by self-governance. The respect the Court has shown for a denomination's autonomy can be seen in *Kedroff*, in which the free exercise right is preserved, not for individuals, but for the appropriate church body. The New York statute was found to violate the First Amendment because it had "directly prohibit[ed] the free exercise of an ecclesiastical right, . . . the church's choice of its hierarchy."[105] The *Barr* court erred in failing to recognize that it is this right of choice that distinguishes religious bodies from all other corporations and private organizations.

The Court's recognition of the rightful autonomy of a religious association is at the core of the "doctrine of judicial deference to a religion's internal decision-making organs."[106] It can be seen in deference in *Watson* to the decisions of church authorities, and in the refusal in *Blue Hull* to permit the departure-from-doctrine test in identifying religious authority. To the extent that *Jones v. Wolf* 1) prohibits judges from interpreting church doctrine, 2) allows only the resolution of secular issues such as property disputes by use of neutral principles of law, and 3) requires identification of the control-

---

[104]Tribe, *supra* n.11, at 876.

[105]344 U.S. 94, 119 (1952).

[106]Tribe, *supra* n.11, at 877.

ling church authority and acceptance of the decision of that body,[107] it stands within the *Watson v. Jones* line of cases.

Judicial deference to the decisions of ecclesiastical authorities was again mandated in *Serbian Eastern Orthodox Diocese v. Milivojevich*.[108] When the defendant Milivojevich was removed as Bishop of the American-Canadian Dioceses by the Holy Assembly of Bishops and Holy Synod of the Serbian Orthodox Church, he brought civil suit against the Mother Church. The Illinois Supreme Court held that the Bishop's removal was arbitrary because it was not held in accordance with the church's constitution, and that it therefore must be set aside. The United States Supreme Court reversed, finding that the detailed scrutiny of the church canons engaged in by the Illinois court interfered with the ecclesiastical decisions of the highest ecclesiastical tribunals of the church. As Justice Brennan put it,

> We have concluded that . . . no "arbitrariness" exception—in the sense of an inquiry whether the decisions of the highest ecclesiastical tribunal of a hierarchical church complied with church laws and regulations—is consistent with the constitutional mandate that civil courts are bound to accept the decisions of the highest judicatories of a religious organization of hierarchical polity on matters of discipline, faith, internal organization, or ecclesiastic rule, custom, or law.[109]

The Court clarified that the First Amendment prohibits judicial inquiry into church procedures for adjudication of ecclesiastical questions. As Justice Brennan paraphrased Justice

---

[107]*See Blue Hull*, 393 U.S. 440, 449 (1969); *Maryland and Virginia Eldership v. Church of God at Sharpsburg*, 396 U.S. 367, 370 (1970).

[108]426 U.S. 696 (1976).

[109]*Id.* at 713.

Miller's opinion in *Watson*, "[A] civil court must accept the ecclesiastical decisions of church tribunals as it finds them."[110]

After *Serbian Orthodox Diocese*, it is likewise clear that First Amendment protection must be applicable to a church's method of government. Just as a civil court may not rule that a church's action is arbitrary because it is inconsistent with the church's constitution, so too a civil court has no authority to determine the extent of jurisdiction of a church. A hierarchy's interpretation of its own laws, doctrines, organization, and regulations is binding on civil courts.

> In short, the First and Fourteenth Amendments permit hierarchical religious organizations to establish their own rules and regulations for internal discipline and government, and to create tribunals for adjudicating disputes over these matters. When this choice is exercised and ecclesiastical tribunals are created to decide disputes over the government and direction of subordinate bodies, the Constitution requires that civil courts accept their decisions as binding upon them.[111]

From this decision one can see the Supreme Court's continuing affirmation of judicial deference toward the decisions of ecclesiastical authorities. The broad prohibition against civil-court interference in religious disputes is firmly based upon First Amendment guarantees. *Serbian Orthodox Diocese* makes clear that if a religious belief is the major issue in a church dispute and if the disagreement over property rights or other secular concerns is a secondary issue, the court must accept the ecclesiastical determination, despite the effect that doctrine might have on the tangential secular matter. If, however, the dominant issue is one of church-property rights, civil courts have a duty to adjudicate them in neutral terms, if at all,

---

[110]*Id.*, referring to 80 U.S. (13 Wall.) 679, 731 (1872).

[111]426 U.S. at 724-25.

without resolving the underlying religious issues. *Serbian Orthodox Diocese* allows no civil determination of issues at the core of ecclesiastical concern, but it leaves open the question of which areas of secular but church-related disputes may be resolved in civil proceedings.

Justice Rehnquist dissented in defense of the Illinois court's procedure for determining a secular but church-related dispute. Both parties had invoked the jurisdiction of the court; each claimed authority over the diocese. The court thus was entitled to determine who was the real bishop of the American-Canadian diocese. Once a court may determine who has authority to decide an issue and what that decision is, it ought, in Justice Rehnquist's view, to be allowed to settle the issue brought before it, without doctrinal preference, as the Illinois court did.

Justice Rehnquist saw the additional step as a difference in degree of judicial participation. The majority, however, saw a clear distinction between the nonintrusive acceptance by the courts of ecclesiastical decisions on religious issues, and the intrusive step beyond that point into the constitutionally protected area of self-determination of religious doctrine and government.

Serbian Orthodox Diocese did not resolve definitively the areas of church life in which civil courts may intervene. Religious organizations are certainly not completely autonomous; they may not claim to be beyond civil jurisdiction simply by presenting religious doctrine to justify their acts. As the dissent in the case suggests, civil courts, in protecting the rights of denominations—by refusing to become entangled in decisions pertaining to religious bodies—may risk denying individuals their fundamental rights.

Justice Rehnquist's concern that individuals not be harmed by unfettered acts of a religious group can also be seen in his opinion in *General Council on Finance and Administration of the United Methodist Church (GCFA) v. Superior Court of*

California,[112] in which he denied a stay of another suit against the GCFA pending the Supreme Court's consideration of the United Methodist Church's petition for a writ of certiorari. He referred to the *Barr* case, to which the *GCFA* case was related, as a purely secular suit, even though the defendant was a religious organization, and then gratuitously added that even religious organizations may not commit frauds upon the public.[113] He also reasserted his view that a civil court may examine a church's internal organization in order to determine a secular issue.

> In my view, applicant plainly is wrong when it asserts that the First and Fourteenth Amendments prevent a civil court from independently examining, and making the ultimate decision regarding, the structure and actual operation of a hierarchical church and its constituent units in an action such as this. There are constitutional limitations on the extent to which a civil court may inquire into and determine matters of ecclesiastical cognizance and polity in adjudicating intrachurch disputes. . . . But this Court has never suggested that those restraints similarly apply outside the context of such intraorganizational disputes. Thus, *Serbian Eastern Orthodox Diocese* and the other cases cited by applicant are not in point.[114]

---

[112]439 U.S. 1355 (1979).

[113]*Id*. at 39, in which Rehnquist, J., quoted *Cantwell v. Connecticut*, 310 U.S. 296, 306 (1940): "Nothing we have said is intended even remotely to imply that, under the cloak of religion, persons may, with impunity, commit *frauds* upon the public." (Emphasis supplied).

[114]*Id*. at 38.

III

Avoiding Liability
and
Protecting the Polity

In deciding ascending liability cases, the courts presumably seek to treat nonprofit organizations no differently than profit-making groups. That is to say, they seek to keep the legal responsibility for obligations of affiliated organizations or the immunization therefrom the same whether the organizations involved are profit or nonprofit. A useful procedure to test that equivalency is to analyze the requirements for a profit and a nonprofit organization wishing to immunize themselves from the liability of an affiliated group.

1. STRUCTURAL SEPARATION

It is elementary that an organization is liable for the debts of its subparts such as divisions and departments. Immunization from liability requires, *inter alia*, that the associated activity or group be established as a separate identity.[1] In the profit sector, this structural separation is ordinarily accomplished by incorporation (with a limited partnership or business trust as alternatives). Incorporation permits the parent organization both to profit and exercise considerable control through stock ownership—to be, if desired, the exclusive owner of the subsidiary. Nevertheless, the parent-shareholder and the subsidiary corporation remain separate legal entities and their relationship is not held to be one of principal and agent.[2]

The sole threat to this structural separation in the profit sector is the doctrine of veil piercing.[3] While the rules of this doctrine are sufficiently vague to permit its application in a broad range of circumstances, it has been employed reluctantly and only in the most egregious situations.[4] In principle,

---

[1]*See* H. Henn & J. Alexander, *Laws of Corporations and Other Business Enterprises* ch. 7 (3d. ed. 1983).

[2]"A corporation does not become an agent of another corporation merely because a majority of its voting shares is held by the other." Restatement (Second) of Agency §14M (1957).

[3]Piercing the corporate veil may be viewed as an umbrella under which a variety of theories—fraud, unjust enrichment, estoppel, agency— might proceed, or as denoting a single idea: that corporate separatenenss will be disregarded when justice requires it. *Taylor v. Standard Gas & Elec. Co.*, 306 U.S. 307 (1939). *See* Note, *Liability of a Corporation for Acts of a Subsidiary or Affiliate*, 71 Harv. L. Rev. 1122 (1958).

[4]"Analysis of the cases has shown that actual fraud need not be shown; the corporate entity may be disregarded when the court finds objective factors indicating misuse of the corporate form, such as the following: outright evasion of contracts and obligations or statutory and regulatory restrictions; a history of spoilation, mismanagement and faithless stewardship which is tantamount to fraud; confusion and co-mingling of assets, or treatment by the parent corporation or shareholder of corporate assets as its own; explicit or implied misrepresentation as to financial responsibility;

formal separations in the profit sector are respected; only in exceptional situations are they ignored.

The same relationship in the nonprofit sector can, superficially, be achieved by one organization separately incorporating its associated activity and becoming its sole member.[5] The Model Nonprofit Corporation Act says that a member of a nonprofit corporation, like a shareholder, "shall not, as such, be liable on [the corporation's] obligations."[6] The parallel, however, breaks down upon closer analysis. Membership, like shareholding, may carry ownership rights (for example, the right to elect directors), but membership, unlike shareholding, generally implies—indeed, is ordinarily entered into for— some form of participation in the activity of the organization. It is the participatory nature of membership that ultimately undermines incorporation of a subsidiary as a relatively safe method for limiting liability in the nonprofit sector. Membership, unlike stock ownership, does not attest to a limited role. The relationship of the member to the corporation is not necessarily antithetical to agency.[7] The actual relation of the

---

direct intervention or participation by the controlling shareholder in the management of the corporation as if it were the business of the shareholder or a division of the business of the parent; failure to maintain adequate corporate records, or ignoring the corporate form by failure to comply with corporate formalities; stripping the corporation of assets, or arranging its affairs so that it has no chance to grow or obtain financial independence; and, last but not least, underfinancing or undercapitalization of the corporation." Hackney & Benson, *Shareholder Liability for Inadequate Capital*, 43 U. Pitt. L. Rev. 837, 850-51 (1982).

[5]The veil of nonprofit corporations can also be pierced. *See* Comment, *Piercing the Nonprofit Corporate Veil*, 66 Marq. L. Rev. 134 (1982).

[6]Model Nonprofit Corporation Act (1964) at § 11.

[7]While the Restatement (Second) of Agency § 14M (1957) expressly notes that agency does not arise from shareholding, it correctly does not so note for membership.

member to the corporation therefore must be examined to determine whether it constitutes an agency.

Moreover, the absence of any limited and defined role for a member and the apparent ease with which unincorporated associations can be judicially created combine to further undermine the subsidiary or affiliate nonprofit corporation as a mechanism for limited liability. The profit parent and subsidiary corporations are not considered one entity simply because their interests and goals are closely aligned. Furthermore, many organizational complexes in the profit sector, such as the Bell group, are recognized as "conglomerates" in which both mutual interests and control exist without mutual agency responsibility. The judicial creation of unincorporated associations based on no more than common purpose and fairness, however, jeopardizes the separateness, and thereby limited responsibility,[8] of aligned nonprofit organizations.

2. FUNCTIONAL SEPARATION

Structural separation is but the first step toward immunization of an organization from the liabilities of its affiliates. Immunity also requires the parties to remain functionally separate.[9]

---

[8]Judicial creation of an unincorporated association is a backdoor approach to potential liability. If the jurisdiction imposes liability on members of unincorporated associations for authorized association activities, as does, for example, California when the association has no officers or management personnel (*Steuer v. Phelps*, 41 Cal. App. 3d 468, 116 Cal. Rptr. 61 [1974]), the creation of an association may well impose liability on the members for the act of another without directly finding an agency relationship between the actor and the members. The creation of the association serves the same purpose as the finding of an agency relationship, but without fulfilling agency prerequisites.

[9]Nothing prohibits, for example, a parent corporation from employ-

As previously discussed, members or sponsors of an organization may be vulnerable as an organization's principals or as its agents. Voluntary participants may prove to be agents by reason of their participation, and the scope of an agency may be broadened by reason of subordination to doctrinal authority (*Stevens v. Roman Catholic Bishop of Fresno*).[10]

Reliable functional separation will probably remain out of the reach of nonprofit organizations unless the legal characterization of their activities is considerably refined. There are no well-defined categories of organizational participation that comfortably exclude agency.

3. REPRESENTATIONAL SEPARATION

An influential factor in the outcome of the retirement-home cases was the weight given to the plaintiffs' real or imagined reliance on the backing of the retirement homes by "the Church." Because of the plaintiffs' circumstances, a sympathetic court or jury could be expected to lean strongly toward imposing ascending liability on little more than nominal representations of connection between the defendants.

Reliance arising from representations of agency can give rise to liability under doctrines of agency by estoppel[11] or apparent authority.[12] Moreover, some recent decisions in the profit sector have imposed ascending liability based on reliance arising from the use of a trade name by a franchisee or

---

ing its subsidiary as an agent. It is not the parent/subsidiary relationship that gives rise to the agency, but the agreement between the separate parties to create an agency.

[10]*See supra*, chapter 1, n. 37; *see also Chellew v. Hope Lutheran Church* and *Allen v. Presbyterian Housing Program*, discussed in chapter 5.

[11]Restatement (Second) of Agency § 8A, (1957).

[12]*Id.* at § 8.

licensee.[13] These reliance doctrines are equally applicable in the profit and nonprofit contexts. Prevailing forms of representing relationships in the nonprofit sector may increase the vulnerability of nonprofit organizations to derivative liability.

Traditional nonprofit terms of relationship, such as "sponsored by," "chapter," "affiliate," "arm," or "agency," carry no standard meaning and may be randomly applied to departments within an organization, to separate agent organizations, or to organizations whose relationships are no closer than a (nonagent) profit subsidiary or sibling affiliate. Moreover, use of another nonprofit organization's generic trade name (for example, Methodism, socialism, or environmentalism) may not require consent and may be intended to signify, not agency, but only a common belief or purpose. Related nonprofit organizations may nevertheless find the representations of their relationships or common beliefs susceptible to an agency interpretation, however unintended and beyond their control.

4. PROTECTING THE POLITY

Two approaches have been suggested for protecting church polity from judicial interference. The first is based on the *Watson v. Jones* rule of judicial abstention.[14] After *Watson* was constitutionalized in *Blue Hull*, state courts could retain jurisdiction over purely secular issues involved in a church dispute, but had to abstain from decisions concerning the underlying religious controversies. The religious issues are to be determined by legitimate church authorities, and the court must defer to those determinations and accept them as given.

---

[13]*See supra*, chapter 1, nn. 94, 97.

[14]*See* Note, *Judicial Intervention in Disputes Over the Use of Church Property,* 75 Harv. L. Rev. 1142, 1154 (1962).

In order to ascertain the legitimate decision-making body, a three-step analysis is to be used. One must first decide whether the denomination is congregational or hierarchical. *Watson* presents these two broad categories, but gives no criteria for making the distinction. Although the choice may be obvious for some denominations, others are not easily classifiable because they have mixed characteristics. An attempt to place denominations with wide blends and varieties of structural patterns into one of two molds does not always lead to a fair analysis of the true polity of those religious associations.

> Reliable indices of control are not easy to come by. The lines of authority within polities are apt to be blurred, and the relevant church law chaotic, voluminous, and unintelligible to a court—even with the aid of expert witnesses. Further, questions of authority are likely to depend on matters of dogma, so that the courts may be drawn into the briar patch of theological controversy from which *Watson* sought to save them.[15]

It seems safe to conclude that in matters of classification of polity, as in the realm of ecclesiastical doctrines, courts should defer to the decision of the competent religious authority within the denomination.

The second step in the analysis concerns disputes between general church authorities and local churches; or between two groups in a congregation, one of which claims loyalty to the hierarchy and the other of which dissents from its policies. The court must decide whether the dissenting church or group is actually within the authority of the church hierarchy—whether it is a related part of the whole church that is subject to the rules and discipline of church tribunals. If a congregation is simply related by name but is otherwise governed independently, then it need not submit to the hierarchy's decisions and control. For example, a Lithuanian con-

---

[15]Note, *Judicial Intervention, supra* n. 14, 75 Harv. L. Rev. at 1160.

gregation that followed the Roman Catholic doctrines of worship bought its own church and selected its own priest without the approval of the Archbishop.[16] The court agreed with the congregation, ruling that the Catholic leader could not claim the church property because the congregation was not in fact an órganic part of the Catholic organization. As evidence in such cases a court must examine the past relationship between the local church and hierarchy: had the congregation been under the control of the general church authority? Although the *Watson* court intended to promote strong, self-governing religious associations by respecting the decisions of their legitimate tribunals, it did not intend "to compel association where none existed before the dispute."[17]

Several approaches by courts to determine if a congregation should be deemed subject to the authority of the hierarchy have proven unsuccessful. Examining the documents that established the local church for evidence of the intention of the church founders or donors is similar to searching for an implied trust and reflects the same flaws. Churches usually begin without following prescribed formalities, but even when a constitution or charter is written, it frequently is not carefully drawn. Nevertheless, when no charter or trust deed is found or no dedication given, some courts have taken that omission not as an oversight, but as an indication that the founders intended the church to be autonomous. This approach should not be used. The intent of the founders usually cannot be known; if it is known, it is often not applicable to the present circumstances of the church. It is apt to be irrelevant, for it takes into account neither development nor the independence of subsequent generations. It is preferable for a court to examine the relationship the individual church and denomina-

---

[16]*Dochkus v. Lithuanian Benefit Society*, 206 Pa. 25, 55 Atl. 779 (1903).

[17]Note, *Judicial Intervention, supra* n. 14, 75 Harv. L. Rev. at 1161.

tion had shortly prior to the dispute. In solving difficult problems concerning religious bodies, a court is more likely to find an equitable balance by using this "living relationship" test rather rather than by interpreting church documents artificially.[18]

Once the legitimate source of authority within a denomination has been determined, the third step is to ensure that the body claiming that authority is in fact the proper body. In a congregational church, for example, the ultimate source of authority is the majority of local church members. Therefore, the court should defer to majority rule in a church convocation. At times courts may intervene to determine which group is the majority, or to decide whether the procedures established by the denomination for its decision making were properly followed. Legal supervision may even be necessary if the dispute is heated or violent. A court-appointed referee may aid in conducting an election or in restoring order so that the duly elected body may act. The court's intervention should only provide stability until anarchy is removed; it must not otherwise interfere.

With hierarchical churches the denomination usually clearly designates the legitimate source of authority. Problems do arise with regard to this designation, however. One example could be seen in the *St. Nicholas Cathedral* cases,[19] in which the Mother Church, the supreme authority of the denomination, was located in a Communist country and the American branch of the church wished to separate. Despite legislative and judicial attempts to validate the assumption of control taken by the American episcopate, the ruling by the Supreme Court insisted that the legitimate authoritative body was the

---

[18]*Id.* at 1162.

[19]*Kedroff v. St. Nicholas Cathedral*, 344 U.S. 94 (1952), and *Kreshik v. St. Nicholas Cathedral*, 363 U.S. 190 (1960).

one with *de facto* control, whether it was located in a Communist country or not. The court's role in hierarchical-church decisions, therefore, is very limited. It may examine the credentials of the tribunal to guarantee that it in fact represents the highest authority in the church. But once it makes that determination, it must accept the decisions of that tribunal. Limited judicial inquiry into hierarchical bodies has been permitted if there is evidence of fraud, collusion, or arbitrariness.[20]

The narrow limitation of judicial review allows those hierarchical bodies with properly vested powers to exercise their control and discipline over the subordinate levels within the church. *Watson* requires this deferential approach. *Kedroff* granted constitutional status to the right of a hierarchical church to appoint its own clergy and to control its property. The Supreme Court would not allow the rebellious American faction to determine the allocation of power and thereby to destroy the true religious judicatory. Instead, the Court guaranteed the freedom to exercise religion by providing for the free functioning of the church's established government.

If either legislative or judicial interference in a church's self-government were permitted, it would affect the free exercise of religion. Among hierarchical churches, the ruling bodies would lose their power to control and to discipline, a power "frequently as fundamental a practice as prayer."[21] Among congregational denominations, governance by the majority, would lose its effectiveness. This loss of control would have a second, less direct but more crucial effect.

> The integrity, autonomy, and stability of a religious association are deeply threatened when the state distorts the association's internal governmental structure. If church

---

[20]*Gonzalez v. Roman Catholic Archbishop*, 280 U.S. 1, 16 (1929).

[21]*See* Note, *Judicial Intervention, supra* n. 14, 75 Harv. L. Rev. at 1182.

property becomes doctrinally encumbered, or the chain of command in a hierarchical polity weakened, the structure of the association is warped. Such a notion was central to *Watson v. Jones*, which the Court in *Kedroff* cited approvingly and which itself rested on policies drawn from the Constitution. True, it is hard to say definitively that religion in America has suffered by reason of disregard of religious associations' autonomy. But such injury is inherently unsusceptible of verification. It would seem enough that the tendency of free intervention is to cause injury, and that the rules of *Watson*, faithfully adhered to, provide a sound prophylactic.[22]

The judiciary, therefore, may determine the proper tribunal for the denomination and may enforce that authority's ecclesiastical decisions. It should not equate religious associations with other private organizations but, because of the delicate policies of noninterference between church and state, rather should treat them as quasi-sovereigns.

The internal functioning of religious bodies, however, is not completely free from judicial review. Courts have considerable discretion in their equitable powers and have even occasionally declined to enforce the decision of a church's authoritative body if they regarded that determination as offensive to public policy or in other ways harsh, unfair, or inequitable. If judicial interference in the decision-making role of denominations were allowed on a frequent or regular basis, it would "debilitate the characteristic functioning of the religious association and so . . . destroy freedom of opportunity to worship as a member of it."[23]

A second approach for guaranteeing constitutional protection to church polity is utilization of the free exercise principle. As suggested above, if the polity of a denomination is a

---

[22]*Id.* at 1183.

[23]*Id.* at 1186.

sincerely held tenet of religious belief, it qualifies for First Amendment protection. The government must then show that its action furthers a compelling state interest and is the least restrictive alternative available. It is clear, for example, that a church's form of religious worship is protected by the free exercise clause of the First Amendment.[24] Jehovah's Witnesses are permitted to distribute their religious tracts, since evangelism is a necessary element of their worship, a purpose or goal that "occupies the same high estate under the First Amendment as do worship in the churches and preaching from the pulpits."[25] The polity of the Jehovah's Witnesses denomination is a key element in the accomplishing of its evangelistic goal.

In fact, a denomination's structure usually is closely related to its form of worship, goal, and purposes; thus, it should be entitled to protection under the free exercise clause. The relationship of a congregation to the general church, and the interaction of different units within a denomination may reflect a church's beliefs, as the doctrine and polity grew from scriptural roots. The distribution of authority in a religious association's strata is crucial in determining the accountability of an individual or a unit within the church. Furthermore, the goals of a denomination are achieved in different ways, depending on the religion's structure. The church's polity is thus a central tenet, recognized in *Watson* as the major element by which to determine the appropriate intervention in church disputes. The self-understanding of a religious body, then, should be accorded the full protection of the First Amendment.

---

[24]*See* Malbin, *Religion and Politics: The Intentions of the Authors of the First Amendment* (1978).

[25]*Murdock v. Pennsylvania* 319 U.S. 105, 108-109 (1943).

IV

CONCLUSIONS
AND
SUGGESTIONS

1. AGENCY

Relationships in the nonprofit sector are not normally confined to a fixed and limited status or level of participation. Due to the multitude of relationships and the variety of potential liabilities, the common-law process, once on the right track, appears to be the best tool for developing appropriate analyses and principles.

Analysis of behalf and benefit concepts in the nonprofit context involves consideration of various activities by individual members and participants and inquiry into whether they are done on behalf of and primarily for the benefit of their nonprofit organization. A distinction must be made between activities of the organization and activities of its members. Often an activity could be on behalf of and for the benefit of either the organization or the member: church members and church agencies engaged in good works or missionary activities, or members and chapters of civil rights organizations pursuing civil rights goals. The issue is whether any agency relationship whatsoever has been established. No inference of agency can be drawn from activities that advance both the actor's and the organization's interests. The presumption should not be one of agency but one of nonagency.

The result should not differ for affiliated organizations and their activities. Local chapters and agencies, engaged in activities similar to those carried on by the national organization, should not be presumed to be acting for the national. Church affiliates, for example, engaging in worship activities or good works, should be presumed to be doing so on their own behalf, absent contrary indications. Nevertheless, courts tend to assume that the activities of local organizations are carried on for the benefit of their national affiliates.[1]

Creation by a nonprofit organization of an affiliate, and retention by the organization of broad policy control over the affiliate, should not work to create an agency or alter-ego relationship. Control of an organization over a nonprofit association not exceeding that of a shareholder over a profit corporation should not give rise to responsibilities beyond those of a shareholder. This principle has been partially recognized for members of labor unions[2] and, in some jurisdictions, for members of other unincorporated associations.[3]

---

[1]*Barr*, 90 Cal. App. 3d 259, 153 Cal. Rptr. 322 (1979), and *Overstreet*, 221 Ga. 16, 142, S.E.2d 816, *cert. granted*, 382 U.S. 937, *cert. dismissed*, 384 U.S. 118 (1965) are two examples.

[2]*Marshall v. I.L. & W. Union*, 57 Cal. 2d 781, 371 P.2d 987 (1962).

[3]Ford, noting that the liability of members must arise under agency

In the case of religious organizations, doctrinal control should not be confused with the control incident to an agency relationship, that is, the right to control conduct. While doctrinal control may amount to agency-like control or coincide with it, often it does not. On occasion doctrinal control may be the only apparent authority. The temptation on these occasions to find agency in doctrinal control should be resisted.

Whether the use of names or relational terms constitutes representation of agency requires independent consideration in the nonprofit context. Public and judicial misconceptions about organizational ties, which are rife among nonprofit organizational complexes, should not give rise to agency responsibility if those misconceptions are neither fostered nor exploited by the organizations. No organization, such as a Baptist Convention, is under a duty to regulate the generic terms of its name, or be responsible for the actions of those who do use such terms. This assertion may, at first blush, appear surprising. We are accustomed to organizations wishing to police the use of their names and marks and thereby assuming any corresponding responsibilities. However, an organization is not required to trademark or otherwise protect its name or any part thereof, nor must it assume, in such a case, any responsibilities inherent in trademark ownership. Moreover, no general legal duty would require a private party to prevent another from creating a confusion of identities. For example, if a "Baptist Nursing Home" was established next door to the "Oak Street Baptist Church"—to which it was

---

principles, classified the membership liability cases based upon the particularity of authorization the member must give. At one end of the spectrum is authorization (and therefore liability arising from membership alone); at the other end, authorization must have been particular to the act giving rise to the liability. H. Ford, *Unincorporated Non-Profit Associations* (1959). The trend in American law appears to be toward the latter view—a view that Ford notes to be a form of limited liability. *See, e.g., White v. Cox*, 17 Cal. App. 3d 324, 95 Cal. Rptr. 259 (1971).

wholly unrelated—the church would be under no legal compulsion to seek to prevent the use of the term *Baptist* by the nursing home or to require some form of disclaimer of relationship, even though the use of the name might lead some people to assume that the nursing home was an agency of the neighboring church.

There seems little reason for nonprofit terms of affiliation, such as "chapter," "agency," or "arm," to be converted to "subsidiary" in order to avoid implying an agency relationship. These terms do not define the legal ties between the organizations, and ought not imply any. The use of identical terms in nonprofits' names often indicates shared beliefs or common ideals and no more.

2. *NONPROFIT SAFE HARBORS*

A nonprofit organization is doubly exposed to liability for the activities of its affiliates—one exposure arising from the possibility of the relationship being held to be one of agency, the other arising from the potential of being merged, along with the affiliate, into a single, unincorporated association with accompanying quasi-partnership responsibilities. A safe harbor is a relationship that will not give rise to liability.

A. *Limited Membership*

Exposure by reason of agency could be curtailed through the establishment of one or more relationships in which control or benefit are, by definition, limited. Simply put, the nonprofit sector needs a counterpart to the shareholder or limited partner. Member status, because it lacks intrinsic limits on its powers or participation, fails to meet this need.

The need could be met through statutory recognition of a class of limited members—members possessing one or more of the following powers, but not others: a vote for the election of directors, a vote on issues of corporate dissolution, consolidation, and merger, a vote on the adoption of the charter and bylaws and amendments, and a vote on statements of corporate belief or position. A limited member could receive benefits from the organization without affecting the limited status. The crux of limited membership is to so limit control that agency is avoided.

Unincorporated associations could be similarly assisted by the statutory creation of an organizational form that might be called a Nonprofit Limited Membership Unincorporated Association. It would parallel the limited partnership, involving control by the limited members and notice to the public. The general partner's counterpart would be the association's officers. Its protection for limited members would not differ markedly from that afforded by the common law in some states,[4] although it would be far more certain.

Limited membership would protect the member from being liable as a principal, but would not bear on the potential of the member to be an agent of the organization. Thus, a sponsoring organization, such as a church denomination, wishing to establish an operating agency over which it would exercise general supervisory control, could accomplish its ends and limit its liability through creation of a separate organization in which the denomination would be a limited member. Benefits received such as an enhanced reputation, would be, as with shareholders or limited partners, irrelevant. An umbrella organization with chapters as limited members, however, would not be protected from ascending liability by reason of the limited membership. The chapters would be protected from being held to be principals, but the umbrella organization would receive no protection from the arrange-

---

[4]A Nonprofit Limited Membership Unincorporated Association would, in effect, codify the common-law trend toward immunizing members of nonprofit, unincorporated associations who have not participated in, or directly authorized, the act giving rise to the liability. See supra n.3.

ment. Appropriate judicial analysis of benefit and control in this situation is the most that can be wished for.

B. Judicial Creation of Unincorporated Associations

Protection from being unexpectedly swept into a single, unincorporated association lies in either a legislative or judicial rule that parallels the creation of a partnership by implication; that is, by requiring an intention to form an association, and some substantive, constituent element of association beyond common purpose. The common purpose/fairness test for creating an association out of concerted nonprofit activity reveals the same weaknesses lodged in the now disfavored joint-enterprise doctrine.[5] Indeed, the underlying issues appear to be much the same. That is to say, judicial creation of a relationship in which liability is extended from one individual to another individual or group—ordinarily an agency relationship—poses peculiar difficulties when the basis for the relationship is nonpecuniary. The joint-enterprise doctrine has all but disappeared with regard to nonpecuniary relationships.[6]

The common purpose/fairness test, however, keeps alive the mistakes of the joint-enterprise doctrine when a nonpecuniary activity is pursued by a larger group. Common purpose alone evidences little in the way of agency or association, and the added test of fairness (that is, whether it is fair that the group should be recognized as an entity), if not begging the issue, reveals nothing but a bankrupt analysis.

Associations are formed, it seems, through the establishment of mutual agency relationships, or through the surrender by members of some degree of sovereignty to the group. It is not enough that two or more individuals happen to be

---

[5]For a discussion of the joint-enterprise doctrine—the doctrine that would impose agency liability on participants in a joint undertaking for pleasure—*see* W. Prosser, *Handbook of the Law of Torts* § 72 (4th ed. 1971).

[6]*Id.* at 477-78.

going in the same direction, or even that they agree to go together if each implicitly retains the power to decide when or
where to depart. It is the surrender of authority and control,
however small, to the group that creates the need for both
group organization and group responsibility. An unincorporated association should not be created judicially by implication
unless the putative members *intend* to surrender some power
to the group.

3. THE CONSTITUTIONAL ISSUES

The four cases litigated after *Barr* suggest that plaintiffs,
by including national denominational structures as necessary
party defendants in civil litigation, are still attempting to per-
suade secular courts to undertake significant reorganization
of religious bodies, even though to do so would offend against
the self-understanding of religious bodies as diverse as the Lu-
therans, Southern Baptists, United Methodists, and United
Presbyterians. From the perspective of the plaintiffs, the de-
vice used to recover on a judgment is hardly novel: the desire
is simply to reach the deepest available pocket to insure that
the plaintiffs' damages will be met. From the perspective of
the religious bodies, however, the issue is not simply a financial
concern, but a constitutional one, involving the right to preserve the self-understanding and autonomy of the religious
body free from external governmental interference. This concern seems clearly warranted by the final disposition of the
Barr case, in which the UMC settled with the plaintiffs at a cost
to the church of more than $21 million.

Religious organizations can count on certain clear judicial
policies. The basic *Watson* rule of judicial abstention is firm:
courts will not determine any religious issues, whether doctrinal beliefs or other ecclesiastical matters, including polity. A
decision by legitimate hierarchical authority concerning the
religious faction that controls a particular church is binding

on civil courts.[7] *Kedroff* has given First Amendment protection to a denomination's autonomy: a church cannot be prohibited from exercising its right to choose its method of governance.[8] *Serbian Orthodox Diocese* mandates that civil courts accept church tribunal decisions with respect to internal organization or ecclesiastical rule without inquiring into that church's adjudicatory procedures or criteria for determining church issues.[9]

In resolving church-property disputes, courts will not impose an implied trust on church assets, nor award the assets to the faction adhering to the fundamental church doctrines. *Blue Hull* presents a very circumscribed role for a civil court. In order not to jeopardize the First Amendment rights of religious bodies, it can apply only "neutral principles of law" in awarding the property.[10] *Jones* went further, and has allowed alternative procedures for deciding these disputes. Courts can investigate all church documents for trust language, and then will award the property either to the party so designated under the express trust, or to the party with legal title.

These decisions appear to warrant the following conclusions: Congregational churches will be assumed to be governed by majority rule, but the majority decision must comply with the church's constitution or other regulations and procedures. The decisions of a hierarchical authority will normally be followed by the court, but not in all instances. The court may, under the "neutral principles of law" standard, review the organizational structure as it would have treated a secular organization, but it may not intrude in internal disputes if the church has its own method for deciding them.

---

[7] 80 U.S. (13 Wall.) 679 (1872).

[8] 344 U.S. 94 (1952).

[9] 426 U.S. 696 (1976).

[10] 393 U.S. 440 (1969).

If the religious body is incorporated, the religious corporation will be evaluated separately from the ecclesiastical body of the church, probably according to general nonprofit corporation rules. Corporate documents will be examined in a "neutral" manner. Religious language and concepts may not be adaptable to such a secular approach, and thus a religious group may choose not to incorporate. Unincorporated religious associations that do not hold documents, however, are at a disadvantage if a dispute arises with a corporate subunit that has articles and bylaws clearly presenting express trusts or other designations that may not accord with the policies of the denomination. Furthermore, an unincorporated organization may be treated like a corporate entity despite its choice of form, as was seen in *Barr*.

Many issues remain unresolved. First, court decisions have not clearly separated the "internal" religious disputes that must be resolved by church tribunals from those realms in which the religious body is not autonomous and in which civil courts may therefore adjudicate. Church-related disputes are often quasi-religious—at what point must those secular issues based upon religious questions be deferred to church authorities? *Kedroff* makes nonjustifiable religious questions that are ancillary or preliminary to another claim.[11] *Blue Hull* makes nonjustifiable all inquiry into doctrinal departures.[12] *Serbian Orthodox Church* makes nonjustifiable any delving into church polity. Justice Rehnquist, however, has stated that these constitutional limitations on inquiry into ecclesiastical cognizance and polity are reserved for intrachurch disputes, but not for secular issues.[13] In *Serbian Orthodox Diocese* and *Barr* there is another element of concern noted by Rehnquist, a desire that individuals

---

[11]344 U.S. 94 (1952).

[12]393 U.S. 440 (1969).

[13]426 U.S. 696, 733 (Rehnquist, J., dissenting).

not be harmed by the acts of religious organizations.[14] If ecclesiastical decisions are completely unassailable, civil courts could
deprive church members of fundamental legal protections that
members of other voluntary associations enjoy. Some social welfare protection is necessary. And thus the unanswered question
remains: when may civil courts intervene?

Second, the body of case law emanating from *Watson* has
codified a simplistic bifurcation of church structure into two
categories, congregational and hierarchical. The polities of
many religious bodies do not fit well into these categories, and
courts are not consistent even when they put a church into one
of these two categories. A more sophisticated and less rigid
method of viewing church governance is necessary.

Third, the actual use of church documents by courts remains unstructured. The majority opinion in *Jones* stated that
a court may examine church documents only to search for language of trust; a search of a church's polity is too intrusive.[15]
In contrast, the dissenting minority insisted that *Watson* and its
lineage dictated that church documents may be considered
only in finding the type of polity of the religious organization;
once the legitimate authority is identified, its decisions are
binding on the courts. In either case, church writings and legal papers will be evidence for the court to consider, and under
the *Jones* decision a state may either follow the presumptive
rule of the majority for voluntary religious associations or may
identify the denomination's controlling unit and follow its decisions. Those denominations that use theological terminol-
ogy throughout their written documents, or that do not
specify clearly the controlling authorities, the relationships

---

[14]*Id. See also General Council on Finance and Administration v. Superior
Court,* 439 U.S. 1355 (1979) (Opinion of Rehnquist, J.).

[15]443 U.S. 595 (1979).

among various subunits, and other ecclesiastical rules and regulations may be harmed by their failure to clarify these matters if they are investigated by courts applying "neutral principles of law."

Court decisions involving a church have been and will continue to be influenced by the church's organizational polity. Increased judicial review of its methods of operation is likely. It is therefore important that religious bodies undertake a careful examination of their structures, so that they may present themselves clearly to courts, the government, and the public. A church's polity normally reflects the religious purposes and beliefs of the denomination; hence, in order to avail itself of the protections of the free exercise clause, the explanation of church structure should clearly reflect the relationship between church polity and religious beliefs.

In any litigation a court will carefully examine a corporate church's articles of incorporation, bylaws, and other documents. They must therefore be written carefully to insure that they faithfully reflect the intended structure and allocation of authority. Standardized pattern language from a legal form book should be avoided because a careful presentation of the religious nature of the corporation could never be captured by traditional legal phrases. The statement of corporate purpose should reflect the religious doctrines and aims of that body. It should not be expressed too narrowly, however, for a restricted or specific statement of purpose may limit later desires to change or expand the denomination's goals.

The documents should be functional, clearly presenting procedures by which decisions are made, but they should also express religious justifications for the sources of authority or the purposes of a particular decision. *Blue Hull* affords constitutional protection to churches in their efforts to define their doctrines, to determine affiliation with other church bodies, and even to change doctrine without judicial imposition of outdated departure-from-doctrine principles. In order to secure this constitutional protection for a religious body, however, the basic documents of that body must formulate clearly the self-understandings the denomination intends to portray.

There is some risk that courts may become more involved in religious affairs if a church has chosen to incorporate. Courts may well distinguish the corporate from the spiritual aspects of a denomination or church organization and then proceed to regulate the corporation because a state-created entity appears more secular in nature and the state feels entitled to control the entity it has created.

By clarifying its structure, the denomination will go a long way towards satisfying the Supreme Court's desire expressed in *Blue Hull* and *Jones* that church documents tell the courts how church-property disputes are to be decided. These documents must be written in such a way that the religious basis for the denomination's governance, objectives, and actions cannot be separated from seemingly "secular" aspects of the church, as construed under "neutral principles of law." The essentially religious character of the church must pervade the descriptions of all aspects of the denomination's self-description. The goal of a religious group is the preservation of its autonomy; it wants to be able to make its own decisions to the greatest degree possible. It must therefore provide to a court invited to exercise jurisdiction over it whatever relevant information the court may need in order to afford to the church the broad First Amendment protection to which it is entitled. This requirement clearly does not mean that a religious body must restructure itself or describe its polity in such a complex or detailed way that a court may find technical error in activities of the church. This clear intertwining of theological justification for a church's governing system may not be easy, but "religious beliefs do not have to be acceptable, logical, consistent, or comprehensible to others in order to merit First Amendment protection."[16]

---

[16]450 U.S. 707 (1981).

The *Barr* case suggests that a change in the tone of the relationship between government and religious groups is imperative. The church and state must rely on one another in today's complex society. If government wants the aid of religious groups, which provide many charitable community programs, those groups cannot be hamstrung by the imposition of massive civil liability because of the contractual obligations or torts of a subunit of the groups, especially where the self-understanding of the religious society must be altered by the government to achieve that end. If the church seeks from the state better understanding of its mission in the world, it will have to express itself more clearly in legal documents affecting its secular life. If, moreover, the church seeks a greater measure of autonomy and self-governance, it will have to acknowledge the legitimacy of the general governmental interest in the prevention of fraud.

Through an attitude of open and mutual respect, the church and the state in the United States can learn to collaborate whenever appropriate and to stay out of the business of the other whenever necessary. And if all this comes to pass, our society will have learned the wisdom of Professor Tribe's suggestion that the religion clauses of the First Amendment "entail a notion of accommodation recognizing that there are necessary relationships between government and religion; that government cannot be indifferent to religion in American life; and that, far from being hostile or very truly indifferent, it may, and sometimes must accommodate its institutions and programs to the religious interests of the people."[17]

---

[17]L. Tribe, *supra* n.153, at 822.

V

LITIGATION IN THE WAKE OF *BARR*

Since *Barr*, four other cases have dealt with judicial consideration of the legal relationships among church units. In all four an agency relationship was alleged by the plaintiff in order to join another church unit or the entire denomination in the suit.

1. THE *CHELLEW* CASE

Chellew v. Hope Lutheran Church is a class-action case with circumstances similar to those in *Barr*. A class of more than seventy-five retired persons sued nineteen Lutheran congregations in the Indianapolis area to obtain monetary damages for alleged breach of contracts between themselves and the Central Indiana Lutheran Retirement Home, Inc. (hereinafter referred to as "Central"). Central was formed in 1974 as an Indiana nonprofit corporation established to provide retirement housing; it closed in 1978 and filed for voluntary bankruptcy in 1980. The plaintiffs are individuals who entered into life-membership contracts with Central and gave Central down payments for apartments in the retirement community called Carmel Creek Manor. Central accepted the down payments but never provided the apartments or refunded the money. The life members, who lost more than $300,000 in down payments and interest, based their suit on the legal theory of actual agency.

> Central is the agent for each and every one of the defendants in this cause of action, who are the joint principals of said agent and who are therefore responsible for Central's actions.[1]

The amended complaint named as defendants nineteen Lutheran congregations that "joined together to establish a community based ministerial program to provide retirement housing to elderly citizens."[2] The complaint did not name as defendants the Lutheran denominations with which the churches were affiliated, and so the *Chellew* case does not present the same issue of ascending liability raised in *Barr*. The congregations are called joint principals, and Central their agent, in the establishment of a retirement community "under the auspices of the Lutheran church and of Central's member congregations."[3]

In their answer, the defendant churches denied the agency relationship and asserted a statutory bar to liability. Under the statutory provision cited, a corporation member is

---

[1]*Chellew v. Hope Lutheran Church*, No. 580-45 (Superior Ct. Boone County, Ind.) Amended Complaint, filed 9 July 1980.

[2]*Id.* ¶ 3.

[3]*Id.* ¶ 27.

liable for the corporation's debts "only to the extent of any unpaid portion of such membership dues . . . or for any other indebtedness owed by him to the corporation."[4] Since no dues or other charges were assessed, the churches argued that they were not liable for Central's debts. These churches were not mentioned in Central's contracts or application forms, and they did not receive payment from Central or from the plaintiff life members of Central. There was no intention that the congregations appoint Central as their agent or that Central intended to accept. Central is clearly a separate entity, argued the churches, and the congregations are simply members of that nonprofit corporation.

The class asserted that the church defendants are accountable under several theories of liability: actual agency, apparent agency, estoppel, and alter ego. The churches held Central out as their agent and themselves out as joint principals of Central, "and are now estopped from denying the agency relationships."[5] They intended to provide a Lutheran retirement home in central Indiana, intended that the project be seen as Lutheran, and often held themselves out as joint agents of Central by giving Central its name and calling it a Lutheran organization, by stating that it was their "joint agency," created to fulfill their social mission to the elderly and to act in accordance with their religious philosophy, by advertising it as "The Lutheran Retirement Home" in their church bulletins and discussing it in those terms at board and congregation meetings, by giving it their membership lists and allowing their members to be solicited for contributions to, and life memberships in, "The Lutheran Retirement Home," and by giving it the unmistakable imprimatur of Lutheran entity from its inception.[6]

---

[4]Indiana Code § 23-7-1.1-7.

[5]*Chellew, supra* n.1, Plaintiffs' Trial Brief at 2.

[6]*Id.* at 8.

Plaintiffs insisted that the relationship between the churches and Central was one of actual agency.

> [T]he strongest evidence of an actual agency relationship is found in Central's articles of incorporation and by-laws of the corporation, which state, in plain and unmistakable language, that Central is a "joint agency" of its participating congregations. This language was drafted by an attorney serving on the ad hoc committee which founded Central. It was expressly ratified by the churches when they approved the articles and by-laws at the organizational meeting. Considered in light of the overwhelming evidence of the churches' involvement in this project and of their *intent* to make it a Lutheran project, there can be no doubt that they intended to and did create a "mere instrumentality" to fulfill their social mission.[7]

The plaintiffs argued that Central was the alter ego of its members' churches, a "mere instrumentality" under the complete control of churches, to be used to fulfill their social mission,[8] that defendants committed a fraud or injustice by leading the plaintiffs to believe that the churches sponsored Central's activities, and that plaintiffs suffered great loss and injustice by placing their trust "in the name and reputation of the Lutheran churches."[9]

Plaintiffs also argued the inapplicability of the affirmative defense raised by the defendants relating to the limited liability of members of a corporation. According to the plaintiffs, the statutory provision on which the defendants relied does not excuse a corporation's shareholders or members from liability under legal theories based on their own conduct apart from their status as members of a corporation.

---

[7]*Id.*

[8]*Id.* at 11.

[9]*Id.*

The central element in the plaintiff class's assertion that the churches must be held liable for Central's contractual breaches was the Lutheran character of the retirement home project.

> The keystone of each of the four theories under which the defendant churches are liable is the significance of the name "Lutheran" and the plaintiff's beliefs that the Carmel Creek Manor retirement project was a Lutheran Home, sponsored by and affiliated with the defendant Lutheran churches.[10]

The plaintiffs' brief lists many widely and publicly accepted uses of organizational names as (1) an embodiment or "personification" of the organization's basic beliefs, attributes, and goals,[11] (2) performing a function similar to a trademark or service mark,[12] and (3) describing a principal attribute of that organization. It is precisely this association by name that plaintiffs asserted bore upon the case at bar.

On 24 May 1982 the jury rendered a verdict in favor of the plaintiff class. The court entered the final judgment regarding the assessment of damages, based on refund of the plaintiffs' down payment with interest for a total of more than $300,000. The case was appealed to the Indiana Court of Appeals, and the three largest Lutheran denominations (The Lutheran Church in America, The Lutheran Church—Missouri Synod, and the American Lutheran Church) jointly filed an amicus brief.

By means of the amicus brief these major denominations, representing thousands of congregations spread over the United States, expressed their concern about the far-reaching

---

[10]*Id.*

[11]*Id.*

[12]*Id.* at 13.

adverse consequences of the trial court judgment on all religious denominations. The denominations argued that the finding of liability was based on a misuse or misunderstanding of the term *Lutheran*, and a misplaced analogy between the use of that term in the title of the retirement home and the use of a brand name or trademark. They also argued that the result of imposition of liability on the churches is certain to have a chilling effect on the social-mission programs of all denominations and congregations.

In support of these claims the brief explained that the word *Lutheran* is a generic reference to a theological and religious doctrine and not, as the trial court erroneously allowed the jury to assume, a reference to a distinctive church entity.

> The term "Lutheran" refers, very broadly, to theological and religious doctrine deriving from the teachings of Martin Luther, and is used by a variety of distinct religious-related organizations which have adopted various of the teachings of Martin Luther. There is no such entity as "The Lutheran Church."[13]

There are eighteen separate Lutheran denominations, each one with a different name, each one autonomous legally, financially, and even theologically. Each has freely adopted its own form of worship and interpretation of religious principles and doctrines. The congregations within these denominations are also separate and function independently. Both the denominations and the congregations are frequently incorporated. The three amicus denominations, for example, are all nonprofit corporations. And their congregations, most of which are incorporated, own their own property, and have their own governing bodies, are exclusively responsible for

---

[13]*Hope Lutheran Church v. Chellew*, No. 1-11082 A 320, (Ct. of App. of Ind.) Brief for the Lutheran Church in America, The Lutheran Church—Missouri Synod, and The American Lutheran Church as Amici Curiae, at 3.

their own debts and liabilities. Because of the legal independence of each denomination and congregation, there can be no principal-agent relationship.

> . . . . It was totally erroneous for the trial court to instruct the jury, as it did, permitting the jury to conclude that the word "Lutheran" denotes a solitary, unified Lutheran church or single denomination. Further, by so misconstruing the word "Lutheran" the court totally ignored the fact that each defendant congregation is a separately organized legal entity. The court's instructions erroneously permitted the jury to find a principal-agent relationship.[14]

The Amici urged that the plaintiffs were incorrect in suggesting that the use of the word *Lutheran* in the title of the retirement home was like a trademark. Within Lutheranism, the term is simply a generic reference to a religious belief and tradition and cannot be owned or controlled, appropriated or registered like a trademark.

The Amici also urged that the liability placed on the Lutheran churches in the *Chellew* case would have many serious consequences. First, its practical effect may be a withdrawal of invaluable church assistance (in terms of financial donations, moral support, and personnel) from many, often irreplaceable, community social-service projects. This removal of social involvement strikes at the very core of the traditional role of all churches. Denominations and congregations have supported organizations engaged in social missions by providing financial grants, consultation, personnel, or representatives on their boards. The relationship between the religious body and the supported organization varies in each case. As the Amici suggested, members of the church give this support as an expression of the principles of their religious faith, social mission, and ministry.

---

[14]*Id.* at 11.

As in the present case, churches supporting humanitarian services rarely expect or derive financial benefit and typically cannot and do not purport to assume financial liability for the projects they may support. Nevertheless, collectively such churches accord great benefits to programs for persons in need, including the aged, in communities throughout the United States.[15]

Finally, the Amici noted that Central was a separately incorporated organization supported by local Lutheran congregations "in carefully defined nonfinancial ways."[16] It is a typical example of the type of support provided to a vast number of separately incorporated social services, many of which do not use the term *Lutheran* in their titles. Neither those social organizations using the word *Lutheran* nor those without it are agents of the denominations or congregations that have provided support. If the term *Lutheran* was used, it refers only to the Lutheran tradition or beliefs in general. Denominations have no power over the generic term *Lutheran*; any social service organization may choose to use it, and no Lutheran congregation or denomination may deny it that right.

Because these repercussions would be harmful not only to the denominations and the social-service organizations that depend on church support but also to the persons they serve, the Amici denominations urged the court to reverse the trial court's judgment.

On 29 March 1984 the Court of Appeals of Indiana, First District, reversed the Boone County Superior Court, holding that no agency relationship existed between the Hope Lutheran Church (and the eighteen other Lutheran churches named in the suit) and the Central Indiana Lutheran Retire-

---

[15]*Id*. at 14.

[16]*Id*. at 15-16.

ment Home, Inc.[17] As the appeals court phrased the issue, "Did the churches' participation in the creation and operation of Central give rise to an actual or apparent agency or agency by estoppel relationship between the parties?"[18] The Court found that no actual agency existed. The plaintiffs had seized upon a provision in Central's articles of incorporation stating that the corporation was a *joint agency* of the participating churches as evidence of actual agency. The court found this use of the term "agency" to indicate that the parties intended only that the retirement home was to be an agency in and of itself, not an "agent" of the participating churches. Thus there was no evidence of an express intention by the parties to establish an agency relationship.

Moreover, actual agency did not exist because the court found that the churches did not exercise control over Central's activities. Central was controlled by its own board of directors; participation by the churches in the formation of the corporation was not tantamount to control. The court rejected the argument of the plaintiffs that the corporation's use of the descriptive term *Lutheran* established an apparent agency. The term was used clearly in a generic sense, the court held, "in an attempt to convey an affiliation with the Lutheran Church in the broadest sense and not a particular congregation."[19]

With respect to the assertion of agency by estoppel, the court noted the complete lack of evidence in the record that the churches had "made false representations or concealed material facts" by permitting use of the term *Lutheran*.[20]

---

[17]460 N.E.2d 1244.

[18]*Id.* at 1247.

[19]*Id.* at 1251.

[20]*Id.*

Such conduct as alleged could not be attributed to the churches because of their previously established lack of control over the corporation. If inaccurate representations were made, they were made by Central, not by the churches. Thus agency by estoppel was inapplicable to the participating churches.

2. THE *ALLEN* CASE

Frank Tyler Allen v. Presbyterian Housing Program, Inc. is a class-action suit filed on 23 September 1982, in the Circuit Court of Johnson County, Indiana.[21] The members of the plaintiff class are approximately three hundred residents of the residential retirement community known as Greenwood Village South (formerly known as Westminster Village South), located in Greenwood, Johnson County, Indiana. They are all elderly persons who purchased a lifetime interest in a retirement apartment or cottage in Greenwood. Each member of the class made a life-occupancy agreement with Presbyterian Housing Program, Inc., an Indiana nonprofit corporation (hereafter referred to as PHP) for an apartment or cottage and for the use of facilities and services at the Westminster Village South Project, (hereafter referred to as WVS), and paid a life-occupancy fee. Alleging breach of those life-occupancy agreements, the plaintiff class filed suit against PHP, its directors and former directors, its officers and former officers, and its employees and agents. Also named were the Synod of Lincoln Trails of the United Presbyterian Church in the United States of America (hereafter referred to as the UPC), the National Retirement Community Consultants, Inc., and others. The

---

[21]*Allen v. Presbyterian Housing Program, Inc.*, No. 33638, (Cir. Ct., Johnson County, Ind.). Complaint filed 23 September 1982. Information relating to the *Allen* case is drawn chiefly from this complaint. In the summer of 1983 the defendants had not yet filed their answer because motions to dismiss had not yet been disposed of.

plaintiff class claimed losses and damages in excess of $1.7 million.

For the purpose of providing a retirement community for the elderly, PHP was formed in 1967. The Synod of Indiana (predecessor of the Synod of Lincoln Trails) paid $15,000 to initiate the project, elected and approved the members of the Board of Directors of PHP, and received annual reports from the Program. The Presbyterian Housing Program was authorized to use the name and logo of the Synod of Lincoln Trails and the United Presbyterian Church to promote Westminster Village South.

The plaintiff residents asserted that they fully and fairly performed their part of the agreements by paying the life-occupancy fees and membership fees. They alleged that PHP breached the life-occupancy agreements (1) by spending more than $1.7 million of the money paid by residents for intended use at WVS on other PHP projects unrelated to WVS, (2) by failing to segregate WVS funds in an escrow account, (3) by failing to maintain WVS property or to provide promised services and facilities, (4) by encumbering WVS property for the benefit of other projects, (5) and by failing to establish and maintain reserve funds to meet debt service requirements.

The plaintiffs alleged that both church defendants (the UPC and the Synod of Lincoln Trails) "fraudulently misrepresented to the Residents that they were related to PHP and financially supported, supervised, and oversaw the affairs and management of PHP, and knew that these misrepresentations were reasonably being relied upon by the Residents to their detriment."[22] PHP, the Synod and the UPC, they alleged, "were agents for each other" in providing housing for the elderly.[23] After representing that they endorsed, supported, and

---

[22]*Id.* ¶ 62.

[23]*Id.* ¶ 79.

supervised the Westminster Village South Project and Presbyterian Housing Program in order to protect the interests of
the residents, and would continue to do so, the Synod and the
UPC failed to maintain its support. In view of the plaintiffs,
the use of the logo of the church defendants in PHP's promotional material created additional liability for the Synod
and the UPC. By authorizing such use, plaintiffs alleged, the
church defendants "impliedly warranted that Presbyterian
Housing Program would be properly managed for the benefits of the Residents."[24]

In summary, the plaintiffs charged that the church defendants, jointly and severally, were liable for PHP's indebtedness and liability as PHP's agents, and are liable for the
breach of representations and covenants, for negligence, and
for fraudulent misrepresentation.

In February of 1983 the UPC filed a Motion to Dismiss
the complaint. In the accompanying memorandum in support of this motion, the UPC is described as "an unincorporated religious union of particular Presbyterian Churches,
organized in a form of government of ascending adjudicato-
ries, with a presbytery over a group of local congregations, a
synod over a group of presbyteries, and an annual General Assembly which controls the entire denomination."[25] It is "organized and governed in accordance with a written
Constitution of The United Presbyterian Church, which includes a written Form of Government and Book of Church
Discipline, as well as other written provisions."[26]

In its motion to dismiss, the denomination urged that it
could not be considered liable for PHP's actions because PHP

---

[24]*Id.* ¶ 82.

[25]*Id.*, Memorandum for the United Presbyterian Church in the United
States of America in Support of Motion to Dismiss at 1.

[26]*Id.*, ¶ 1.

had used a particular religious symbol. The UPC also urged that it should be dismissed on the ground that it could not be held liable for PHP's actions on the strength of an initial donation when the nonprofit corporation was formed, and that it should not be held accountable for the actions of PHP since the conduct at issue in the case involved only the plaintiffs and the separately incorporated PHP. Finally, the denomination raised constitutional grounds for its dismissal as a party defendant, urging that imposition of liability on the church would violate both the Indiana Constitution[27] and the free exercise clause of the First Amendment to the United States Constitution.

In its memorandum the UPC expanded on these justifications for dismissal. The allegations of denominational responsibility for the housing corporation's actions was premised on two facts: first, that the Synod of Lincoln Trails made an initial contribution to the housing corporation; and second, that the denomination "either permitted, or failed to prevent, the use on promotional literature of the symbol or 'logo' [indicating affiliation with The United Presbyterian Church]."[28]

The UPC argued that neither fact yields the conclusion that a religious denomination should be held liable for the obligations of a subunit. The UPC memorandum noted that recoveries against the religious organization for the acts of a sponsored program have occasionally been allowed when actual or apparent agency has been shown or when disregard of the corporate entity has been justified, but noted that "the facts of the situation, as alleged in the complaint, do not allow a recovery."[29]

---

[27]Ind. Const., art. I ¶¶ 2, 3, 4.

[28]*Allen*, No. 33638, Memorandum of United Presbyterian Church, at 1.

[29]*Id*. at 2.

With respect to the use of the denominational logo, the UPC argued that Indiana law "requires a manifestation by the principal to the third party, on which the party reasonably relies" as a proof of apparent agency, and that PHP's use of the church logo cannot be considered such a manifestation.[30] It is not a symbol designating a limited warranty but rather "indicates merely an affiliation with the Church which, absent something more, is not sufficient to establish liability on the part of the entire denomination for the obligations of a separately-incorporated unit."[31]

Finally, the UPC urged that the distinct character of the separately incorporated entities should not be disregarded. The UPC noted that the plaintiffs alleged neither an upstream transfer of assets from PHP to the Synod or the denomination nor such complete control over the affairs of PHP by the Synod or the denomination that it is a mere instrumentality or adjunct of the Synod or the denomination itself. The church defendants concluded that they should be dismissed from the *Allen* case because neither the agency theory nor the corporate veil-piercing theory can be sustained on the facts alleged in the complaint.

In the summer of 1983 the *Allen* case was still in the preliminary stage of pretrial pleadings. Together with the *Chellew* case, it could forge a resolution of the ascending liability issue in the Indiana tribunals different from that reached by the appellate court in *Barr*.

3. THE *BOZEMAN HOSPITAL* CASE

In 1978 the Board of Trustees of a hospital in Bozeman, Montana, known as the Bozeman Deaconess Foundation (hereafter referred to as the BDF) restated its articles of in-

---

[30]*Id.* at 3.

[31]*Id.*

corporation so that its Board of Trustees had no affiliation with the United Methodist Church and so that its property was no longer held in trust on behalf of the church. The only mention of any connection with the Methodist denomination in the new document was found at the end of the paragraph on title to property: at the time of dissolution of the corporation, consideration was to be given "to the investments and financial support of the Yellowstone Conference."[32]

The Yellowstone Conference of the United Methodist Church, a nonprofit Montana corporation, responded to these new articles by challenging the authority of the BDF's Board of Trustees. It sought and won an injunction against the BDF's adoption of new resolutions or filing of the restated articles. Immediately thereafter, in June of 1978, the BDF, also a Montana nonprofit corporation, filed an action to quiet the title to its property; it named both the Yellowstone Conference and the United Methodist Church as defendants in a quiet-title action.

BDF alleged that the United Methodist Church was "not a corporate or other legal entity in the State of Montana and has offices out of Montana, the location of which is not now known," and that its authorized agent, the Yellowstone Conference, had no valid interest in the plaintiff's real personal property."[33] Noting that the Annual Conference was of the view that the trustees of the hospital held the property of BDF in trust for the Yellowstone Conference and that they could not legally amend the articles of incorporation in the manner proposed in 1978, BDF maintained, nonetheless, that they were the lawful owners and possessors of the property and

---

[32]*Bozeman Deaconess Foundation v. Yellowstone Conference of the United Methodist Church.*, No. 24566, (District Ct., Gallatin County, Montana) Restated Articles of Incorporation of Bozeman Deaconess Foundation, at 4, *as cited in* Exhibit C appended to Complaint filed 29 June 1978.

[33]*Id.*, Complaint, at 1.

that they had amended the Articles properly by a greater than two-thirds vote of the members of the corporation at an annual meeting.[34] The District Court rejected this claim, issuing a restraining order enjoining the filing of the 1978 version of the articles of incorporation. Hence, the plaintiffs brought a subsequent action to quiet title to its property and to file its restated articles.[35]

Service was attempted upon Bishop Ralph A. Alton, Bishop of the South Indiana Annual Conference of the United Methodist Church and President of the Council of Bishops of the UMC, on behalf of the UMC. Bishop Alton moved to dismiss the action against the UMC or, in the alternative, to quash service of process.[36] Bishop Allen argued that "the United Methodist Church is not a jural entity capable of suing or being sued."[37] Bishop Alton set forth the history of the denomination, describing its governmental structure as neither hierarchical nor congregational, but rather loosely connectional. The Bishop pointed out those elements of the denomination, also mentioned in the *Barr* defense, that make it unique: the considerable autonomy of local churches and a large worldwide denomination with no central headquarters, no offices, and no employees.

The Alton brief argued that the United Methodist Church is not, and cannot be, an "unincorporated association" under Montana law, since the State's statutes offer no definition nor list of criteria for such an entity. The brief argued further that a body can be found to be an unincorporated association only if it has control over its members, at least

---

[34]*Id.* at 2-3.

[35]*Id.* at 4.

[36]*Id.*, Consolidated Motions, at 1.

[37]*Id.*, Brief in Support of Consolidated Motions, at 1.

with regard to the sphere of activity involved in the issues being litigated, and that this kind of control was not present in the UMC. The brief acknowledged that courts have occasionally accorded jural status to unincorporated associations, citing *United Mine Workers v. Coronado Coal Co.*,[38] which held that a union was a suable entity because of its purpose and organizational structure, the power of its officers, and the corporate-type structure of its financial transactions. According to the Alton brief, *United Mine Workers* is readily distinguishable because the UMC has a loose connectional system rather than a tight organizational structure, there is no chief executive or governing board controlling the affairs of the whole denomination, and the General Conference operates as a legislative, not administrative, body for only two weeks every four years.

Neither does it have an agency relationship with its component boards, agencies, and affiliated institutions. No member or unit of the denomination has the authority to bind another in responsibility. Citing case authority requiring "a showing of 'association responsibility' of all members, through internal agency delegation by Constitution, by-laws, agreement, or similar delegations, to reach the association common funds,"[39] the brief argued that since this requirement cannot be met in these circumstances, the UMC cannot be held to be a suable jural entity.

The Alton brief argued that bringing the UMC into court as a legal entity would breach the denomination's First Amendment freedoms by denying it the right to establish and maintain its own structure, because:

> (a) it would be an attempt to radically alter the internal structure of the UMC or "disestablish" its established pol-

---

[38]259 U.S. 344 (1921).

[39]*Bozeman*, No. 24566, Brief in Support of Consolidated Motions at 22.

120   MERCER STUDIES IN LAW AND RELIGION

ity, and (b) it would impair the free exercise of United
Methodism and other faiths by discouraging the future
identification of the denomination, by name, in the affairs
of local units, ministries, and programs.[40]

Local churches and church-related organizations would be
obliged to remove the name "United Methodist" and to sever
or restructure their relationship with Methodism in order to
avert liability and litigation. Other denominations would be
forced to follow suit. The brief argued that the "chilling
effect"[41] that reorganizations of church polity would have on
the church would constitute a separate violation of constitutional principles.

    In reply to the claim that the UMC is not a legal entity, the
plaintiffs relied on the determination to the contrary by the
California Court of Appeals in *Barr*.[42] Plaintiffs' counsel,
moreover, urged the Montana court to attach greater significance to the denial of certiorari in *Barr* than is warranted.[43]

> Since the highest Court of the land has *approved* the
> finding that the United Methodist Church is a legal entity,
> . . . I believe this Court should make the same finding.[44]

    The Yellowstone Conference noted correctly that the *Barr*
court's determination of the jural status of the UMC was based

---

[40]*Id.*

[41]*Id.* at 30-32.

[42]*Id.*, Plaintiffs' Brief in Opposition, at 2.

[43]A denial of certiorari is not an indication that the Supreme Court approved of the decision in the case or affirms its judgment, but only that
fewer than four Justices deemed the case worth review on the merits. *See,
e.g., Maryland v. Baltimore Radio Show*, 338 U.S. 912 (1950) (Opinion of
Frankfurter, J.) and discussion in R. Stern and E. Gressman, *Supreme Court
Practice* 353-60 (5th ed. 1978).

[44]*Bozeman*, Plaintiffs' Brief, *supra* n.39, at 8 (emphasis supplied).

upon the California Code of Civil Procedure.[45] Montana, however, has not amended its rules of civil procedure governing suits against business associations but has kept the form of the statute originally found in California before the amendment.[46] The two statutes are substantially different; the Montana law does not even mention unincorporated associations. Hence the defendant Annual Conference argued:

> [S]ince the two sections are not the same, and [since] the *Barr* case is based upon the California [Code], as amended, the *Barr* case based on the amended California Code . . . cannot be used as authority in Montana to support its position that the Defendant United Methodist Church exists as a jural entity.[47]

Bishop Alton submitted a supplemental brief, arguing that the UMC should be dismissed as a party (1) because it is not a jural entity, (2) because the court lacks jurisdiction over the UMC, and (3) because the UMC cannot claim any property interest in the BDF property.[48] This brief attempted to clarify the meaning of the provisions in BDF's charter that the plaintiffs believed might cloud their title to BDF's property, namely, the standard "trust clause" requiring that upon dissolution the proceeds would be held in trust for the use of the Annual Conference. According to the supplemental brief, the phrase, "according to the usages in the Discipline of said church," only indicates that the proceeds should be supportive of the church's religious interests.

---

[45]*Bozeman*, No. 24566, Brief in Opposition to Bozeman Deaconess Foundation's Motion for Summary Judgment, filed 16 May 1980, at 1-2.

[46]*Id.* at 2.

[47]*Id. at 2-3.*

[48]*Bozeman*, No. 24566, Supplemental Brief of Ralph T. Alton, filed 22 August 1980.

... The qualifying words seized upon by plaintiff concerning "the usages of the Discipline of said Church" do not identify a secondary trustee or ultimate beneficiary or any United Methodist title-holding entity other than the Montana not-for-profit Annual Conference, The Yellowstone Conference.[49]

The supplemental brief urged that the court accept the uncontested testimony of religious experts and Methodist leaders concerning the church's structure. The brief pointed out that "the language and usages of churchmen may be quite different from the language of courts or from usual secular interpretations of words,"[50] and that for this reason civil courts must respect and accept the interpretations of ecclesiastical experts in understanding church law and polity. The supplemental brief further argued that the UMC should be dismissed because the ecclesiastical authority of the church, the *Book of Discipline*, as interpreted by three experts in Methodist polity, makes clear that the UMC is not a jural entity.[51] Noting that ignoring the correctional character of Methodist polity would be to "interfere with the very essence of Methodism by imposing structure where there is none,"[52] the brief concluded:

> Since the structure or polity of an organization is often directly connected with the philosophy of an organization, The United Methodist Church must be free to define itself and its structure in any way it sees fit. If, as a result there is no centrally focused organization which in effect is The United Methodist Church, but rather The United Methodist Church is comprised of a series of in-

---

[49]*Id.* at 2-3.

[50]*Id.* at 9.

[51]*Id.* at 10-13.

[52]*Id.* at 15.

dependent, autonomous connectional sections, it must be accepted by the courts.[53]

The supplemental brief assailed the *Barr* case as "[t]he only case in this country in 200 years which has ignored the First Amendment and ignored the structure of the [Methodist] church" and described *Barr* as "a faulty decision which in time will be reversed if voluntary organizations and religious denominations are to have any future."[54]

On 22 December 1980, Judge Peter G. Meloy denied the plaintiffs' motion for summary judgment and dismissed Bishop Alton from the *Bozeman Hospital* case. On 21 January 1981 Judge Meloy also dismissed the United Methodist Church as a party defendant. The Judge issued a lengthy opinion accompanying his December 1980 order dismissing Bishop Alton. In this opinion he summarized the evidence relating to the nonauthoritative character of the Council of Bishops (of which Bishop Alton was president at the time of the attempted service),[55] the connectional character of Methodist polity as set forth in the *Book of Discipline*,[56] and the nonincorporated status of the denomination.[57] As Judge Meloy summed up the evidence,

> [The United Methodist Church] is, in short, the name given to a large collection of local churches and other organizations comprising a major Protestant religious faith.[58]

---

[53]*Id*. at 16.

[54]*Id*. at 17-18.

[55]*Bozeman*, No. 24566, Opinion and Order Granting the Motion to Dismiss of Bishop Ralph T. Alton, Dec. 22, 1980, at 2.

[56]*Id*. at 3.

[57]*Id*.

[58]*Id*.

Judge Meloy also noted that the Bishop could not act as a legal representative for the UMC, nor could anyone, and that service upon him was thus insufficient. Nevertheless, the Yellowstone Conference, as a nonprofit corporation, had full capacity to sue and be sued.

> It is the proper organization to assert any interests affecting United Methodism which may arise in this case.[59]

Judge Meloy addressed the "severe limitations" placed on civil courts by the First Amendment in the resolution of church-property disputes. Summarizing the *Watson* line, the judge concluded:

> Most importantly, the First Amendment prohibits civil courts from resolving such disputes on the basis of religious doctrine and practice. Civil courts are required to defer to the resolution of issues of religious doctrine or polity by the highest court of a hierarchical church organization. The state may adopt the "neutral principles of law" approach when this is consistent with constitutional principles or when the controversy involves no consideration of doctrinal matter.[60]

The court had requested both sides of the dispute to provide references to the *Book of Discipline* in support of their positions concerning the status of the UMC as a jural entity and concerning the title to BDF property. The defendants' counsel submitted both excerpts from the *Book of Discipline* and affidavits from church authorities, which the court "weighed against Plaintiff's bare and unsupported assertion that The

---

[59]*Id.*

[60]*Id.* at 4.

United Methodist Church is a jural entity capable of being subjected to the jurisdiction of the Court."[61]

For Judge Meloy, the answer to the question "What is the United Methodist Church?" is to be determined not on the basis of "neutral principles of law," but on the basis of the church's self-understanding as reflected in the *Book of Discipline* and as interpreted by authorities of the church. Those authorities, in their affidavits, unanimously asserted that the UMC is not a jural entity or an unincorporated association, and the court's role is simply to follow their lead.

Judge Meloy also addressed the "chilling effect" issue, noting that judicial meddling with denominational polity could cause great harm.

> This Court is also mindful of the dangers inherent in judicial contradiction of a religious faith's structure and organization according to the faith's own understanding of itself. If courts were free to interfere with the organizational structure of religious societies, classifying them for litigation purposes in ways which offend the actual form in which the members chose to effectuate their religious beliefs, the threat to all organized religious faith would be obvious.[62]

The Judge noted, nevertheless, that relief might still be sought against individual, autonomous units within the denomination.

> Indeed, in this case the appropriate regional unit, the Yellowstone Annual Conference, is before the Court and any and all legal or equitable rights to the Bozeman Deaconess properties should be properly asserted by that entity.[63]

---

[61]*Id*. at 5.

[62]*Id*. at 5-6.

[63]*Id*. at 7.

For these reasons the Court dismissed the UMC from the lawsuit.

> This Court is convinced that to subject them [the individual persons and church units] to jurisdiction would violate the "establishment" clauses of the Montana Constitution (Article II, Section 5) and the First Amendment to the Constitution of the United States. For purposes of this action there is no "United Methodist Church" which is a national jural entity capable of suing and being sued. The proper party, if any, is the Yellowstone Conference of the United Methodist Church, a Montana corporation which is already joined as a Defendant in this action.[64]

In March 1981 the remaining parties reached a settlement agreement. Under the settlement the BDF rescinded its restated articles and reinstated the 1961 amended articles with some further amendments. Perhaps the most significant amendment was an addition to the articles of incorporation stating that the Yellowstone Conference is the beneficiary of the trust created in the property, but that its interest in the trust could not be liable to the claims of others. Another significant change required all proposed amendments of the BDF's articles of incorporation to be submitted to the annual meeting of the Yellowstone Conference "to determine if the proposed change meets the requirements of the Discipline of the United Methodist Church."[65]

On 9 March 1981, the District Court accepted the settlement and ordered the case dismissed with prejudice.[66]

---

[64]*Id.* at 7-8.

[65]*Bozeman*, No. 24566, Stipulation for Dismissal, Jan. 28, 1981, at 4.

[66]*Bozeman*, No. 24566, Order, March 9, 1981.

4. THE *MINOR* CASE

In April 1981, Barbara H. Minor filed a Title VII sex-discrimination suit against the Southern Baptist Convention, the Brotherhood Commission of the Southern Baptist Convention, and three individual defendants in the United States District Court for the Western District of Tennessee.[67]

Minor is a secretary who alleged in her complaint that she was hired both by the Southern Baptist Convention and by the Brotherhood Commission, which she characterized as "an agency" of the Convention.[68] She alleged that she was offered a promotion and increase in salary by the defendant David Haney if she would take business trips out of town with him. In May 1980, Minor accompanied Haney to a "Lay-Renewal" convention as part of her new duties as divisional secretary and "up-front girl."[69] Minor alleged that her employer was guilty of sexual harrassment.

> During the course of that trip it became apparent to the complainant that the defendant Haney intended that sexual favors were to be a part of the requirements of the position as "up-front girl" as well. During the course of that trip sexually insulting remarks were made by the defendant Haney and an attempt was made by Haney to arrange and foster an adulterous sexual relationship between the complainant and another employee of the Southern Baptist Convention. The complainant refused.[70]

---

[67]*Minor v. Southern Baptist Convention*, Cir. No. 81-2309-H, Complaint filed 9 April 1981.

[68]*Id.* ¶ 21.

[69]*Id.* ¶ 24.

[70]*Id.* ¶ 25.

Minor alleged further that Haney's sexually suggestive comments and solicitations of other employees of the Southern Baptist Convention continued and that her repeated refusals led to increasingly intolerable working considerations. Soon after telling Haney that such treatment must not be a condition of her employment, the plaintiff was informed that she would not get the promotion or raise. Minor stated that she reported Haney's conduct to various officials within the Brotherhood Commission and the Southern Baptist Convention but that none of them took any action that she deemed appropriate. Finally, Minor alleged that she had suffered psychological harm, damage to her reputation, invasion of privacy, and economic losses because of the actions and omissions of the defendants. She sought declaratory and injunctive relief, as well as damages.

The Southern Baptist Convention (hereafter referred to as the SBC) moved to be dismissed from Minor's action for lack of subject matter and personal jurisdiction and for failure to state a claim upon which relief can be granted. Dr. Harold Bennett, the Secretary/Treasurer of the Convention, described the structures of the SBC and the Brotherhood Commission in an affidavit attached to this motion. Dr. Bennett explained that the SBC is a Georgia nonprofit religious corporation with six officers, none of whom is an employee of the SBC. Although acknowledging that the SBC is a jural entity, Bennett stated that it actually is "best characterized as a church related body."[71] The Convention, he stated, employs no one.

The Brotherhood Commission is an autonomous, separately incorporated, body controlled only by its own directors. No officers of the SBC serve as directors, officers, or employees of the Commission, nor is there any "control by the Con-

---

[71]*Id.* Affidavit in Support of Defendant, Southern Baptist Convention's Motions to Dismiss, at 2.

vention of the employment practices of the Brotherhood Commission of the Southern Baptist Convention."[72] The Brotherhood Commission owns its own property and assets.[73] Although it is an institution that receives funds from the churches that attend the annual Convention, the SBC does not control the Commission's use of the financial support.

The annual Convention is the meeting at which Baptists from all over the United States gather for a few days "to pool their resources for the promotion of Christian missions, education, and benevolent enterprises which they believe serve the Kingdom of God."[74] Approximately 4,000 churches that have previously contributed to the religious ministries send "messengers" to the annual Convention. The Convention is a "loose confederation of churches" that determines how the combined gifts of the churches are to be used that year to spread the gospel of Jesus Christ.

> This is a Convention of "messengers" (not delegates). The churches do not belong to the Convention. There are no member churches.
> These churches do not sign or confess to a creed. They need not be related to any other Baptist group. Their ministers need not be "approved."[75]

Once the Convention's messengers determine the distribution of financial support, those institutions receiving aid are free to use the money as they choose. The Brotherhood Commission is just such an institution engaged in religious ministry. Its decision to employ or promote the plaintiff Barbara Minor (or not to do so) was its own, "and its actions were

---

[72]*Id.* at 4.

[73]*Id.* at 6.

[74]*Id.* at 5.

[75]*Id.*

without the knowledge, consent, approval, or support of the Convention or its officers."[76]

In a memorandum supporting the motion of the SBC to dismiss, the Convention argued that it does not fall within the statutory definition of an "employer" in Title VII,[77] since it has no employees and since the Brotherhood Commission is a completely separate corporation with its own employees and its own employment practices.

> The Court may not consolidate the two corporations for the purpose of applying Title VII to the Southern Baptist Convention under any integrated enterprise theory. There is no interrelation of operation, common management, common financial control, or centralized and common control of labor relations. . . .[78]

The SBC invoked the religion clauses of the First Amendment, urging that any state interference with the denomination's polity would be unconstitutional.

> Any joinder by the Court of the two corporations would be an interpretation and distortion of church polity and administrative governance as established by the Southern Baptist Convention and would offend the establishment and free exercise provisions of the Constitution. There can be no state ruling invading the right of the church to determine its control and form of church government.[79]

---

[76]*Id.* at 6.

[77]"The term employer means a person engaged in an industry affecting commerce who has fifteen or more employees." 42 U.S.C. 2000 e(b) (1976).

[78]*Minor*, No. 81-2309-H, Memorandum in Support of the Motion of Southern Baptist Convention to Dismiss, at 2.

[79]*Id.* 3-4.

In an out-of-court settlement between the parties, the defendants agreed to pay Mrs. Minor $25,000, and on 18 June 1982 the Federal District Court ordered the settlement agreement binding.[80]

The *Minor* court never had to intimate its own views on the relationship between the SBC and the BC or on the important First Amendment issues raised by the SBC. *Minor* thus does not confirm the *Barr* precedent, but serves to illustrate how skillful advocacy can avoid legal interpretations harmful to religious bodies. Although no presentation of the theological background of the Baptist denomination was offered in the Convention's Memorandum or in Dr. Bennett's Affidavit, the latter document offered to the court a thorough explanation of the functioning of the annual Convention. The use of the term *messengers* is important, for messengers bring the decisions of their churches to the Convention. In other words, the source of power originates with the individual, autonomous, local churches, and not with the Convention. Therefore the individuals who attend the convention are not delegates to a decision-making body, but rather messengers bringing decisions already made. In this sense, the Baptist denomination is indeed a loose confederation of churches. The messengers, by democratic process, decide how the collected

[80]*Minor*, No. 81-2309-H, Order Finding Settlement Agreement Binding on Plaintiff and Enforcing Its Execution. In this order the court found that Mrs. Minor had agreed to the settlement and had signed the letter from defendant's attorney concerning the agreement. Despite her husband's disapproval and despite Mrs. Minor's contention that "there was never a meeting of the minds" between herself and her attorney, the court was convinced that Mrs. Minor authorized and agreed to the negotiation of a settlement and understood the terms of the agreement. *Id*. at 4-5. After finding the plaintiff's attorney's actions to be above reproach and the terms of the settlement fair, that court concluded that the settlement "constitutes a binding agreement and should be enforced." *Id*. at 6. As of the summer of 1983 this judgment of the District Court was pending on appeal.

contributions are to be distributed to various organizations. To be sure, this pooling together indicates an interrelationship, but not a hierarchical one, or one in which an agency relationship can be shown to exist. Once the messengers determine how their churches' gifts are to be distributed to institutions, those institutions are free to use the funds they receive with no control or right to control within the Convention.

Even more than Methodists, Baptists have historically reflected a profound theological commitment to autonomy of the local congregation. Perhaps this is one reason why the *Minor* court did not follow *Barr* in redefining a religious community in a manner foreign to its own self-understanding. Had it done so, it is clear that it would have been in violation of the constitutional principle against excessive governmental entanglement in religious matters that was articulated in *Watson* and its progeny.

APPENDIX:

THREE DENOMINATIONAL PERSPECTIVES ON ASCENDING LIABILITY

1. The Methodist Approach*

If someone has a complaint, and wanted to go to the head of The United Methodist Church with it, that head person would be hard to find. One might try the president of the Council of Bishops, but would discover that this person is primarily a presiding officer over the semiannual meetings of the Council of Bishops. The president has no particular authority in the church at large not possessed by all other bishops. . . .

This is simply to illustrate that power and authority are widely dispersed within The United Methodist Church, undoubtedly deliberately so. We have inherited from the founders of America a rather keen distrust of too much power centralized in one person. There is not only not a head person, there are no headquarters of our church. This is not necessarily bad, but we should recognize that this general lack of central direction over the years has resulted in our various boards and agencies pretty

---

*Prepared by Kent M. Weeks.

much going their own independent ways. . . . Bishop Tuell, *The Organization of The United Methodist Church*, (rev. ed. 1977)

How do Methodists see themselves in the aftermath of the *Barr* litigation? The question was never whether The United Methodist Church existed. It existed and continues to exist as a connection of about ten million members in more than 45,000 local churches affiliated with 114 annual conferences in the United States and abroad. Methodists have always held that theirs is a connectional church, its structure neither hierarchical nor congregational. That structure was at the core of the dispute in *Barr*.

Of the various defendants, only The United Methodist Church sought to be dismissed from the litigation. The essential question in *Barr* was whether an international religious denomination, such as the United Methodist Church, with thousands of constituent churches, conferences, and units serving in connection, can collectively be held accountable for the acts of a local unit or charitable corporation that may be related to any of its 114 annual conferences.

The essential holding of *Barr* was that while churches can be protected from court intervention in internal matters, they cannot be protected in matters involving a secular dispute. The court found that the church had entered the secular world; thus, their actions were subject to court review.

In response, United Methodist Church leaders turned their attention to the relationships of various agencies to church bodies, sometimes severing ties and sometimes thoughtfully reassessing and restructuring relationships. The Pacific and Southwest Annual Conference immediately severed ties with its various agencies and informed them that they should not claim a relationship to the Conference and should not use the word "agency" in any of their documents. Trustees of Bozeman Hospital in Montana attempted to separate the hospital from its supporting Methodist Conference, apparently with the intention of freeing the hospital from any church agency so that the hospital's assets could not be attached in the event of an unfavorable outcome in *Barr*. Church lawyers moved to dismiss The United Methodist Church as a party to the litigation and the court ruled that indeed the church had none of the attributes of an unincorporated association. Eventually a settlement was reached. The *Bozeman Hospital* case is fully discussed in chapter 5.

Unfortunately for the church, *Barr* has called to the attention of potential litigants the possibility that church units can be sued.

Nevertheless, a court in North Carolina has found that The United Methodist Church does not have the characteristics of a quasi-corporation.

> The connectional system of United Methodism does not parallel and bears no similarity to the required organizational and administrative forms which courts of this and other states have held to be essential to any treatment of an association of commonly named persons as a separate jural entity with capacity to sue and be sued (*Hinson v. The Methodist Retirement Homes,* 1981).

A somewhat more calm approach has been taken by several church agencies. For example, the Board of Global Ministries, (a defendant in *Barr*) accredits hospitals within the United Methodist system and maintains guidelines in retirement homes that claim a relationship to The United Methodist Church. The agency has now reviewed its relationships with the various hospitals and retirement homes that it accredits and has issued a very detailed guidebook on the relationships.

Another agency of the church has established a committee to review and assess the *Book of Discipline*. The committee, composed of lawyers, lay people, and several bishops, has reviewed the *Book of Discipline* as it relates to the denomination in light of *Barr*. The committee has recommended specific changes that will ultimately be reviewed by the General Conference of the United Methodist Church when it meets in 1984.

Other church agencies and institutions such as hospitals, colleges, and retirement homes are now working to identify and clarify their relationships. These church agencies are not walking away from a relationship but are asserting that if they are related in a way that might generate liability they should take responsibility for that relationship.

Many United Methodist-related colleges have initiated conversations about their relationships with their sponsoring Annual Conferences. Most United Methodist colleges are related to Annual Conferences, although for historical reasons the twelve predominantly black institutions are related to the General Board of Higher Education and Ministry of the United Methodist Church. The colleges and church representatives are focusing on three basic questions: What is the relationship? What should the relationship be? And how should that relationship be structured? Specifically, church conferences and colleges are considering the following questions: Does the mission statement of the institution define its church relationship? How is this statement operational in the life of the college? Does the church body support the colleges in finances and student recruitment? What does the college charter say about the selection of members of the board of trustees by the Conference? Who has formal title to college property? Does the board of trustees receive information necessary to make informed decisions? In some cases, after thorough exploration of these and many other issues, covenants have been written and procedures regarding trustee selection, property ownership, and the mutual responsibilities of college and church have been spelled out with greater precision.

It is heartening to see many church units taking on the task of reevaluation with vigor and optimism. Clearly, they understand that undefined terms such as *agency*, which may have one meaning within the church and quite a different meaning in a court of law, must now be defined. Relationships must be worked out between Annual Conferences and institutions, which must include understandings, preferably written, about financial obligations. The church documents should be reviewed by lawyers to make sure that the language in the documents clearly states what is intended and does not subject the church body to unwarranted legal interpretation unintended by the drafters. Once the agreements have been worked out, they must be accurately and fully described to the public. Finally, of course, the litigation points to the need for good management of church-related agencies so that the problems arising in California do not occur again. The problems there were extreme, and few, if any, agencies would be vulnerable to the potential difficulties presented by the inability to fulfill life-care contracts. The homes are now operating effectively, to the great relief of the members of the Conference. Few, if any, of the persons in the homes were harmed by the bankruptcy proceedings or the class-action suit.

For many churches, not only The United Methodist Church, the critical issue in *Barr* was the lurking First Amendment issue. Essentially the question was whether the California Court of Appeals made a determination contrary to expert testimony and the Church's internal ecclesiastical interpretation in violation of the First Amendment's protection of the right of free exercise of religion.

Since the United States Supreme Court refused to review the decisions of the California courts, it never addressed the First

Amendment issue. The California Court of Appeal, however, did address the issue and found that it was not applicable to the case because the case involved The United Methodist Church's external bodies. Therefore, the issues were not matters of internal church polity. But even so, the prospect of courts redesigning the polity of the church, as the California court did, in order to make it conform to legal reasoning and case law is disturbing for all churches. In the future, church polity must be written so that there is no possibility for misinterpretation by the courts. And similarly, church bodies and their related institutions must clarify their relationships in unambiguous language and make sure that the substance of those relationships reflect reality and competent legal assessment.

2. The Lutheran Approach*

The Lutheran Church—Missouri Synod (the "Synod"), not unlike other church bodies of substantial size, watched carefully as the *Barr* case unfolded. The Synod sought to use the allegations and strategies applied by both the plaintiffs and the defendants, as well as the outcome of the case, to "fine-tune" its relationships with many entities, the activities of which could result in ascending liability to the Synod. In fact, by the time the *Barr* litigation had begun, the Synod had made substantial progress in recharacterizing its relationships with those entities that form a part of the synodical union and those that, although commonly identified with it, are independent organizations not accountable to the Synod.

The Synod is the second largest Lutheran denomination in North America and is, despite its name, an international church body. It was established by German immigrants in the late 1830s. By 1854, it had established itself regionally within the United States. The German immigrants who established the Synod also established a theological seminary, now Concordia Seminary, at St. Louis. Subsequently, the Synod established or acquired other educational institutions in order to train its full-time elementary school workers. (Congregations that are members of the Synod operate more elementary schools in the United States than any other church body except the Roman Catholic Church.) The Synod's educational system now consists of three theological seminaries and twelve colleges and junior colleges.

---

*Prepared by Philip E. Draheim.

In addition to the districts and educational institutions, the Synod has established a publishing house, a foundation, an archives, and an organization through which money is borrowed from individuals in order to finance acquisition or construction of church and school facilities for member congregations. These entities, as well as the districts and educational institutions, all exist as corporations established under the laws of the states or provinces in which they exist. These corporate component parts of the Synod are termed "synodical entities."

All of the synodical entities are governed by the Synod's Constitution and the Bylaws. It is in this respect that they are distinguishable from the approximately 6,000 member congregations, all of which are autonomous and most of which are incorporated. It is also in this respect that they are distinguishable from the scores of other entities, many of which are engaged in "social ministry," that are often identified with the Synod. Nevertheless, during the late 1960s it became obvious that there had been considerable blurring of the relationships of the Synod to the synodical entities and to the other organizations identified with the Synod but not a part of it. Within five years the relationships had been substantially clarified; by mid-1979, the last step had been taken in this process.

The process, as completed, was to identify those organizations actually outside the Synod and not subject to its Constitution but nevertheless recognized by it in some way. These were labeled as either "auxiliaries" or "listed service organizations." The relationships between the Synod and these organizations are authorized by a synodical bylaw. In the case of listed service organizations, the status is governed by a formal agreement between the Synod and each organization. Both the bylaws provisions and the formal agreements clearly specify the relationship as one in which the Synod is not responsible for the activities of the organization, especially not for its debts and liabilities. They also obligate the organization to publicize this fact in certain specific situations in which there is significant risk of potential legal liability.

Creating the "listed service organization" status was the last step in the procedure. The initial step, applied only to "social ministry" organizations, was to change what had previously been the form for recognition by the Synod of these organizations. To understand the metamorphosis, it is necessary to know a bit about the history of the social ministry organizations affected.

In most situations, social-ministry organizations (homes for orphans, residences for the handicapped, facilities for the elderly, hospitals, child and family counseling services, and so forth), were established by member congregations of the Synod in a particular metropolitan area or locality. These social-ministry organizations, like the Synod itself, were established by local congregations, which maintained ultimate control. From an early date the member congregations of the Synod authorized and directed the appropriate boards and staff members of the Synod to provide certain kinds of assistance to the social-ministry organizations when requested and to serve as a clearinghouse for information passing among them. Yet at no time has the Synod been put in a position of being able to direct or control the social-ministry organizations. Despite this, the close contact between the respective organizations and the Synod and its districts gradually developed into a relationship pursuant to which the Synod accredited the organizations whose programs it had reviewed and determined worthwhile. It and the organizations freely referred to this accreditation, and referred to the organizations as "agencies" of the Synod. No requirements were imposed on the organizations or staff members of the Synod and its districts to communicate to parties with which the organizations dealt, through contracts or otherwise, that the organizations were independent and solely responsible for their own debts and other liabilities. An examination of the articles of incorporation and bylaws of the social ministry organizations usually would have established this independence. Nevertheless, notions that were either expressed or could reasonably be implied from the activities of Synod officials and officials of the organizations often served to obfuscate this independent status.

Efforts to reach agreement with other national Lutheran church bodies on how to deal with the situation were complicated. These other church bodies had also experienced the establishment of social-ministry organizations, sometimes by their member congregations but also, in many cases, by the national church bodies or their judicatories. With respect to a church body like the Lutheran Church in America—the largest Lutheran church body in North America developed by the mergers of formerly independent Lutheran church bodies—there was a variety of historical relationships with social-ministry organizations. During the 1950's and 1960's, many social-ministry organizations had become "pan-Lutheran" and had relationships with two or more of the national church bodies. It was, therefore, difficult, if not impossible, for the organizations to communicate adequately their relationship with the national church bodies with which they were identified because different religious principles and organizational experiences existed among them.

After a series of meetings, the national church bodies were able to agree that the relationships between those church bodies and the social-ministry organizations should be governed by a set of criteria, pursuant to which the organizations would be "endorsed" for "affiliation" with those church bodies choosing to so affiliate with one or more of them. The matter of "endorsement" was handled as a private matter by the organizations and represented the cooperative effort of the major national church bodies under the name "Lutheran Social Service System." If, upon review, a particular social-ministry organization was endorsed by the Lutheran Social Service System, then each national church body would determine separately whether it wished to establish an "affiliated" relationship with the organization. If so, it would enter into an agreement with the organization. Included among the endorsement criteria, and as a provision in the affiliation agreement, was the requirement that each organization acknowledge that it was solely responsible for its debts and other liabilities—none of which were the responsibility of a church body with which it might affiliate—and that it would appropriately communicate this fact in instances where there was a significant risk of legal liability.

Coincidentally, during this same period of time (the early 1970s), the status of synodical entities was also scrutinized by the Synod. A doctrinal controversy within the Synod erupted, and a large portion of the faculty and student body of the Synod's Concordia Seminary in St. Louis established a "seminary-in-exile." A small portion of the Synod's congregations terminated their membership in the Synod in sympathy with the views leading to the seminary-in-exile, and the presidents of a few of the Synod's districts actively supported the seminary-in-exile.

Although the Synod had never been a federation of districts but rather had always been an organization that established its districts for its own convenience, the day-to-day working relationship between the districts and the congregations assigned to those districts could easily create the impression that the congregations had established the districts. Under such a view, an argument could be made that the districts and their assets should be identified with the congregations, which, as previously noted, are autonomous.

As a result of this potential challenge to the structural integrity of the Synod, it became necessary to clarify the historic relationships. The Synod now portrays more clearly which entities are within the synodical union (though existing as corporations) and are subject to its constitution and bylaws. An important part of this effort has been to prevent existing synodical entities from establishing yet other corporations unless certain precise requirements are satisfied, thus blocking any major increase in the number of synodical entities. This practice established a basis for identifying objectively those organizations that are actually a part of the Synod. This identification is essential to distinguish them from entities that only appear to be a part of the Synod or accountable to it (and for which the Synod, in turn, may be held accountable). The purposes to be accomplished by religious bodies, and the persons most active in the functions of those bodies, provide strong impetus for the creation of all kinds of entities, quasi-entities, and alliances. When this tendency is left unchecked, it is virtually impossible to comprehend the cast of characters and their relationships to each other.

The Synod has followed this process with complete awareness that in many cases the result may be to diminish or eliminate the protection from legal liability that might otherwise be afforded by corporate status. In some cases, as for example where a synodical entity offers and issues debt securities for its "church extension" purposes, protection against the entire Synod becoming financially obliged is sought. This protection is accomplished through provisions in the debt instruments and through use of offering circulars that clearly state that creditors are entitled to look only to the assets of the particular synodical entity corporation for repayment. There are no obligations or guaranties by the Synod generally or by any of its other parts. In other cases, however, this avenue of defense has been relinquished in favor of a better perception of the organization, leading to a greater predictability and, therefore, the opportunity for better risk management.

The dual clarification of the status of synodical entities and the recognition of only those nonsynodical entities listed as service organizations provide a strong defense to ascending liability. Synodical officials are vigilant to ensure that expressed and implied expectations of parties are consistent with the status of the particular entity involved. Of course, there cannot be complete assurance of nonliability if the Synod and the other entities are to be able to function effectively, but this "business risk" is accepted because of the relatively high degree of predictability offered by the structural relationships.

3. The Southern Baptist Approach*

Who are the organizations in the phenomenon loosely called "the Southern Baptists"? They are:

1. The local church: a congregation of believers.
2. Organizations related to that church, such as its Sunday school or day-care center.
3. Baptist general bodies
   a. Associations
   b. State conventions
   c. Southern Baptist Convention
4. Organizations related to one of these general bodies.

The *church* in Southern Baptist polity is the local congregation. It may be an unincorporated association or a legal corporation, but it is totally autonomous. The congregation alone controls its faith and practice. It creates itself, ends itself, ordains its ministers, employs whom it will, controls its finances, establishes its ordinances, grants membership to whom it pleases, and relates to other churches and general Baptist bodies in a manner of its own choice. There is no hierarchical doctrinal control in the Southern Baptist system.

The *association* was the earliest of Southern Baptist interchurch organizations. It is generally composed of churches in an area (perhaps a county) that choose to associate. Associations may or may not allow a church to associate depending upon the association's assessment of the faith and practice of the church. Thus, both the association and the church are free to relate or not. If they relate, neither surrenders autonomy. Whether the church chooses to associate within its local association or whether the association chooses to include the church within the fellowship of the association has no bearing on any relationship the church might choose to have with the Southern Baptist Convention or with a state Baptist

---

*Prepared by James P. Guenther.

convention. The association's activities are generally "missionary." The organization is not usually incorporated, and its activities are controlled by messengers from the associated churches.

A *state convention* is an organization that may or may not be incorporated. The state conventions meet annually and are composed of messengers elected by those churches voluntarily cooperating with the state conventions. The church is not controlled by the state convention. The constitution (Article 1) of the Baptist General Convention of Texas is typical in stating that the state convention "has not, to any degree, and shall never have any ecclesiastical authority. It shall not have and shall never attempt to exercise a single attribute of power or authority over any church or over the messengers of the churches in such wise to limit the sovereignty of the churches, but shall recognize the sovereignty of the churches under one sovereign, Jesus Christ, our Lord."

The state convention insists on its own autonomy as vigorously as the state convention defends the autonomy of the local church. The convention chooses its own membership and is sovereign within the bounds set by its own constitution. Therefore, just as it controls no church, no church or group of churches controls the state convention. The concept of messenger control of general Baptist bodies is firmly planted in Southern Baptist history and practice. Autonomy is so important that Southern Baptists guard against even the appearance of its compromise. Therefore, churches and general Baptist bodies legally relate only through the medium of messengers.

Most state conventions support colleges, orphanages, and other benevolent institutions and religious ministries. They engage in various "programs," such as promotion and missions.

The *Southern Baptist Convention* is the largest of the general bodies. It is incorporated. Those churches in the United States who are in "friendly cooperation with" and "sympathetic with" (Constitution of the Southern Baptist Convention, article III) the purposes of the Southern Baptist Convention may send messengers who constitute the membership of the annual convention. Whether the church is eligible to send messengers depends upon whether the church has contributed money to the convention in the fiscal year. Thus the relationship between the church and the Southern Baptist Convention is established by the church's choice. The Southern Baptist Convention has no faith and practice test for churches or for the messengers of churches. Nor does the Convention exercise authority over any other Baptist body.

The messengers elect the Southern Baptist Convention's committees and officers and the board members of the various corporate institutions directly related to the Convention. The messengers also determine how monies received by the Southern Baptist Convention during the following year will be parceled out to various institutions.

The Convention has no property and no employees. It does not exist in any corporeal sense except during the four days each year when the messengers constitute the Convention.

The *Cooperative Program*, though a concept and not an organization, deserves description. It is the name given to a joint financial appeal made by the Southern Baptist Convention and individual state conventions to individuals through their churches. The budgets set by the messengers at the state convention and at the Southern Baptist Convention are presented to church members as worthy of financial support. The members of the local churches are asked by the Cooperative Program fund-raising efforts to include "The Cooperative Program" in their church's budget. Thus, when a member in one of these churches contributes a dollar to his church, he knows in advance the percentages of his dollar that will go to his church, to each beneficiary institution of the state convention, and to the Southern Baptist Convention.

The church budget controls how much of the dollar goes into the Cooperative Program stream. The messengers to the state convention have already determined what percentage of Cooperative Program receipts from churches will be used in the state; the balance moves on to the institutions of the Southern Baptist Convention according to percentages previously determined by the messengers constituting the last annual Southern Baptist Convention.

Churches and/or individuals are free to choose not to include the Cooperative Program in their stewardship strategy. Churches or members may designate their gifts. For instance, they may exclude a particular state beneficiary or include only certain institutions both at the state and Southern Baptist Convention levels. Thus the church, the state convention, and the Southern Baptist Convention have each maintained their autonomy. The church may choose not to participate in the Cooperative Program and may still be eligible to send messengers both to the state convention and the Southern

Baptist Convention. State conventions, as well as the Southern Baptist Convention, are free to drop out of the Cooperative Program.

Legal title to the money, once given to the Cooperative Program, is in the church, the state convention, and the Southern Baptist Convention, respectively, at the various stages of the process. The equitable title is in the institutions of the state conventions and Southern Baptist Convention according to their distributive percentages.

Institutions are related either to a state convention or to the Southern Baptist Convention. All Southern Baptist Convention and most state convention institutions are incorporated. Their affairs are controlled by corporate directors elected by the respective convention's messengers. The institutions receive none, some, or most of their income via the Cooperative Program. They present their requests and needs to the appropriate committee of their convention which in turn recommends the percentage allocations to the messengers at the convention.

Because the church is neither above nor below the general bodies, Southern Baptist organizations are a community of autonomous entities, sharing only a common purpose. Thus, the principal legal theories that impute the liability of one organization to another are difficult to apply to the various relationships between organizations in Southern Baptist life.

Parent-subsidiary. The Southern Baptist Convention is a corporation. Each of the institutions related to it is a separate corporation. Their legal relationship is akin to that of a parent corporation (the Southern Baptist Convention) to its subsidiary (the Foreign Mission Board of the Southern Baptist Convention, for instance).

When will the law require the parent to pay the debt of its subsidiary or pay damages to an injured party because of a tort or wrong committed by the subsidiary? If the two corporations operate as if they were one corporation, then the courts will treat them that way. The courts look for the extent of domination and control by the parent over the subsidiary.

The only Southern Baptist relationship remotely resembling parent-subsidiary is that of the convention to the institution. No church holds the power to control the election of the directors of any other group and no other group holds any power to control the church as a corporation. Nor is one general body governed by any other general body. (The parent-subsidiary model is not, however, applicable to the state convention-Southern Baptist Convention relationship. There is no legal interconnection between these groups—no method whereby one can control the selection of directors of the other.)

In what ways does the convention dominate the institutions related to it? The convention (be it state or Southern Baptist) typically provides funds to the institution and requires it to operate in conformity with a business and financial plan. That plan requires prudent financial practices and spells out the budget process and requirements of financial reporting. Further, the constitutive instruments of the convention generally require that institutions related to it have their charters approved by the convention or its executive committee. Officers of the institution are, in the case of the Southern Baptist Convention, required to be members of co-operating Baptist churches.

The institutions adopt their own bylaws. The affairs of the institutional corporation are exclusively in the hands of the directors of the corporation, and they elect the officers of the institution. All matters of employment are in the control of the institution's directors. The Southern Baptist Convention's charter, constitution, and bylaws recite no creedal constraints on the institutions related to Southern Baptist Convention (save for a constitutional requirement that the Foreign Mission Board only appoint missionaries "who furnish evidence of piety, zeal for the Master's kingdom, conviction of truth as held by Baptists, and talents for missionary service" (Article IX).

The Convention holds no power to dismiss a trustee during his term. The institution owns its own property and maintains its own accounts and books. It may sue or be sued, contract, borrow, pledge the assets of the institution, or mortgage the institution's real estate. The constitutive instruments of the Southern Baptist Convention make clear the Convention's intent that the institutions are to be controlled by the institution's own trustees.

Agency. Just as a parent corporation is not liable for the acts of the subsidiary simply because the parent controls the election of the subsidiary's directors, the power to elect the subsidiary's directors does not make the subsidiary the agent of the principal (Restatement of the Law, Agency, 2d, § 44M).

Analysis under the "benefit and control" approach to agency relationships in the case of the Southern Baptist Convention is unfruitful. The principle is that the work of the agent is for the benefit of the principal and is subject to its control. The concept that "he who gets the benefit ought to be liable for the risks taken" developed in the law of profit and commerce. It is foreign in the context of religious work and ministries. When, for example, the Foreign Mission Board heals the sick, digs a well, and teaches the illiterate, the Southern Baptist Convention does not realistically receive the benefit. The recipient is clearly the beneficiary. It is impossible that benefit would come to any proposed "principal" as the result of the act of any suggested "agent" in the ministries of the churches or of any convention's organization.

Agency exists when both benefit *and control* are present in the relationship. The foregoing has explored the question of control and found such to be generally lacking in the Southern Baptist relationships.

Master-servant. Under this theory the master is liable for the tortious act of his servant if the tort was committed within the scope of the servant's employment (*respondeat superior*). A custodian, for instance, is a servant of his church; if he commits a tort in the course of his employment (leaves a waxed floor in a slick condition), the church may be liable for injuries that result.

On occasion, courts have determined that ministers are servants not only of the local church but also of the minister's order or the denomination. In those cases, the courts have looked at the extent of control held by the denomination over the minister. In the Southern Baptist context ministers are not controlled by the Southern Baptist Convention, a state convention, nor any association. A local congregation determines whether a minister is to be ordained, what minister they will employ, and the terms of his employment. There are no denominational criteria, no doctrinal control, no bishop, and no placement system. While servanthood is an important part of the minister's role, he clearly is not the servant of any general Baptist body.

Whenever Southern Baptist organizations have found themselves defendants, they have asked that their polity be respected and that their congregational, nonhierarchical structure be understood. So far there has been no imputation of liability from one organization to another that has offended Southern Baptists' understanding of themselves.